'I am so happy to endorse *Unleashed*, the book which unpacks the theme of Spring Harvest in 2020, by Gavin and Anne Calver. It is packed with biblical insights about how the early church in Acts inspires us to be all the Lord wants his church to be today. It is challenging and honest. If we live out this teaching it has the potential to transform our nation. And, as for the authors, they live this out in their everyday lives!'
Debra Green, OBE, National Director and Founder of Redeeming Our Communities (ROC).

'In a matter of decades, the early Church grew from that handful of frightened fishermen hiding in a Jerusalem prayer room to the dominant sociopolitical and spiritual force in the Roman world. The detonation of this movement is recorded, of course, in the Acts of the Apostles—brilliantly explored, expounded, and applied in Gavin and Anne Calver's new book. Skillfully they unleash the power of the Gospel, the potential of the Church and the extraordinary possibilities of the age in which we live. This is dangerous stuff!'
Pete Greig, 24-7 International and Emmaus Rd, Guildford

'I started reading *Unleashed* to write an endorsement but was soon gripped, inspired, and deeply challenged. The story of the early Church in the book of Acts shows us our Christian roots and the values of early believers. It challenges current ministry paradigms and practices and calls us back to the way of the Holy Spirit. I would encourage you to read slowly and pause to pray often, and ask the Lord to open your eyes to see the truth and your heart to feel the way he feels. *Unleashed* is spiritually challenging and very practical. This book will help you live a life unleashed. Thank you, Gavin and Anne, for this precious gift.'
Steve Uppal, Senior Leader, All Nations, Wolverhampton

D0260295

Gavin and Anne Calver live in London and have two children. Anne is the associate minister at Stanmore Baptist Church, and Gavin is the CEO of the Evangelical Alliance. They both previously worked for Youth for Christ and currently serve on the Spring Harvest planning group, which Gavin chairs. Ordained Baptist ministers, authors, and regular public speakers, they have a deep desire to see the UK transformed for Christ. Away from ministry, they are keen runners and football fans with Anne supporting Liverpool and Gavin AFC Wimbledon.

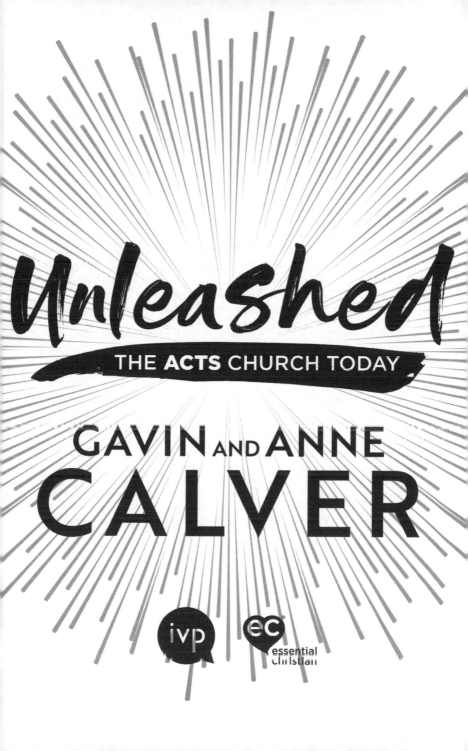

Unleashed

THE **ACTS** CHURCH TODAY

GAVIN AND ANNE
CALVER

ivp

ec
essential
christian

INTER-VARSITY PRESS
36 Causton Street, London SW1P 4ST, England
Email: ivp@ivpbooks.com
Website: www.ivpbooks.com

ISBN: 978-1-78974-136-0
eBook ISBN: 978-1-78974-137-7

Typeset by Nord Compo

Printed and bound in Great Britain by Ashford Colour Press Ltd, Gosport, Hampshire

*Inter-Varsity Press publishes Christian books that are true to the Bible and that
communicate the gospel, develop discipleship and strengthen the church for its
mission in the world.*

*IVP originated within the Inter-Varsity Fellowship, now the Universities and Colleges
Christian Fellowship, a student movement connecting Christian Unions in universities and
colleges throughout Great Britain, and a member movement of the International Fellowship
of Evangelical Students. Website: www.uccf.org.uk. That historic association is maintained,
and all senior IVP staff and committee members subscribe to the UCCF Basis of Faith.*

To the Church . . .

for the Church . . .

in the confidence that one day we will be the bride that the Lord longs for us to be.

We have loved writing this book and have felt hugely challenged by the idea of being 'unleashed' ourselves. We long to see a real move of God in this land and are desperate to play our part in this. We are grateful for many friends who've helped us on this journey, especially those who contributed their stories to this book or read earlier manuscripts and were so helpful in their feedback.

This is not the full story of the church in Acts and is certainly not a Bible commentary; it's the story of a number of pivotal moments in the early church that hold great relevance today. We're not telling the full story but hoping that you will be inspired by what we have covered and long to read the wider book of Acts as a result. We are focusing on chapters 1–12, which present the way that the church began. Chapters 13–28 offer a case study in church development by using the story of Paul. Acts as a book is not fully concluded and so we today are living out Acts 29.

As co-authors, we have both contributed to every chapter. When the story in the chapter ends, the writer may well change, but be assured that every sentence has been agreed together.

Enjoy the ride!

Gavin and Anne

Contents

Part 1
UNLEASHED POWER

Acts 2:1–21

Part 2
UNLEASHED PEOPLE

Acts 2:42–47 and 4:32–37

Contents

Part 3
UNLEASHED PRESENCE

Acts 5:12–25

Part 4
UNLEASHED POTENTIAL

Acts 8:4–8 and 26–40

Part 5
UNLEASHED PARTICIPATORS

Acts 12:1–17

Foreword

To try to be the church without the continual empowerment of the Holy Spirit is like trying to breathe without lungs. We, the church, are utterly dependent upon God's presence and power. We need God's wisdom to speak truth into a post-truth society. We need God's grace to demonstrate love and acceptance to a society that is open to Jesus, but not always open to his people. We need God to give us courage to proclaim a gospel that is hopeful enough to bring forgiveness to those who seek it, and strong enough to enable transformation in the lives of individuals from the inside out. In short, we need the Spirit's power to enable us to be God's people in God's world. There has never been a greater need for the Church of Jesus Christ in the United Kingdom to come back to the hopeful, inspiring, and life-shaping message of the book of Acts. We do not need to replicate the early church, but in the words of St Paul, we need to be reminded that 'the same power lives in us' as lived in those early believers.

Unleashed invites us to move forward by remembering who God is, what God wants to do in the world, and the power by which God will bring about his purposes. Anne and Gavin Calver have written a book that reminds us that we do not need more big plans, or ideas, or strategies if we are to see the kingdom extended. Their book reminds us that we do not need 'more' of anything. Instead, they call us to remember that God needs more of us. Their words will sound like a song in the soul of anyone who longs to see a greater move of the Holy Spirit. *Unleashed* invites us to dream again of what God can do with Christians who willingly lay their lives and their futures before God for heaven's purposes. This book is more than a brief reflection on the book of Acts. It is an invitation into a life that

xv

is abandoned to God. It is a call to all of us who long to see God's kingdom come and his will be done, on earth as it is in heaven. My prayer is that we not only read it, but we encounter God through it and let his Spirit and his power propel us into his mission in our communities and our world.

May God unleash his power in us, then unleash His people into the world.

Rev Malcolm J. Duncan, FRSA
Theologian-in-Residence for Spring Harvest and Essential Christian
Lead Pastor of Dundonald Elim Church
Author, Broadcaster, and Theologian

Premise

'Without a sense of urgency, desire loses its value.'

Jim Rohn

Over the last few years we have felt an increased sense of urgency in our guts. We know that we join many in longing that God's kingdom would come and his will be done in our nation. Darkness covers the land, and yet the eyes of the Lord range throughout the earth looking for hearts and minds that are fully committed to him (2 Chronicles 16:9). He longs to pour out his spirit on his people for the extension of the gospel, and we are desperate to partner with him to see more salvation, healings, transformation, and repentance. Light is shining in the dark. There is hope, and he has a name: Jesus.

This book is born out of a passion to see the church rise up ever more and move more fully into the call of God. When we have begun to dig into the Acts narrative, we start to feel a sense of unease; the church of the New Testament looks, sounds, and appears so seemingly different from much of the church of the United Kingdom. When we talk church here in Great Britain, our immediate thoughts can easily relate to buildings and services on a Sunday. If you had talked church in first-century Ephesus, they would have thought of a band of rebels who were healing people and roaming the streets declaring the Resurrected Lord. When we think of the church here in Britain, we can easily find ourselves thinking of a sermon, coffee in polystyrene cups, and worship dependent on a projector.

If you look at the Acts church, it was a group of people empowered by the Holy Spirit, sharing everything they had and being family in a way that seems alien to the majority of us. The Acts church does not refer to buildings or to how long a service should be, and it doesn't spend time critiquing the worship style or arguing about hierarchy and the validity of ordained ministers. The Acts church is about people—each and every individual, all empowered differently as the body of Christ to carry hope into the community, into their homes, and everywhere they found themselves.

In many ways we read the book of Acts and think it is an impossible dream to imagine the Acts church at work in the UK today, but we believe in a God of the impossible. He is not limited by our human understanding, and he promised to do even greater things through us before he returns for his bride. This book is about dreaming together of how we can see a transformed church. It is about drawing on the stories of others who have seen the Holy Spirit move in great power, who have obediently stepped out and watched Jesus transform the people around them, here and beyond.

These words are written to awaken and challenge us afresh to consider how we can draw more of the lost, the broken, the outcast, the rich, and the poor into the kingdom. We will talk about the reality of the everyday, because we live in it and we acknowledge that perhaps not every model in Acts is applicable today. However, what we do see is that the gospel spread rapidly, and the believers were one in heart and mind, ministering in words, works, and wonders. We may not live in great persecution, but what if we did? How important is our personal walk with Jesus?

We have called this book *Unleashed* because it was prophetically birthed on retreat with the Spring Harvest team—a time when God led us into deep repentance and longing for his bride. We emerged with an even greater yearning for transformation, awakening, and empowering and knowing that if Spring Harvest could be one catalyst to equip the church towards more of the mission of the King, it was worth a try. We asked the question 'Which bit of your word is right for this, Lord?' We knew without a doubt that it was Acts: the Acts church today. What underpins the entire journey through Acts? The power of the Holy Spirit.

We cannot write this book without acknowledging that the key ingredient for God's people to do his work is more of the Holy Spirit. This is a yearning in our own hearts and for all of his children. May this exploration through some of the book of Acts lead us all into a life-changing encounter with the Living God that transforms his ministry in us and through us, alongside others, in Jesus' name.

Introduction

'On five occasions in history the Church has gone to the dogs, but on each occasion, it was the dogs that died.'

G.K. Chesterton

As young people, church was a struggle for us both. This was certainly as much our fault as anyone else's, but this didn't ease the struggle in any way. We'd sit there passively listening to someone speak for what felt like an eternity, stand to sing dispassionately when told to, and long for the whole thing to be over so we could chat with our friends. With hindsight, we are sure it was never quite as bad as this, but as teenagers our experience of church so often felt safe, sanitized, and disengaging.

Over the years that have followed, we have often found ourselves in church settings where it feels like things could really happen, but for whatever reason, the congregation have got the spiritual handbrake on. For all that the Lord might want to do, we would rather not lose what makes us feel safe and, ultimately, what we control. The problem is that when you pursue comfort, you get comfortable magnolia contexts. When you follow calling, you get vision and direction. We have found ourselves often asking: Is there not more than this? Is this really how church should be? Was it like this in the time of the New Testament?

Fast forward a few years to a time when we both sat in a familiar spot: the front row of the Skyline at Minehead. We love Spring Harvest and were having a great week being blown away by all the Lord was doing. The theme of 'Only the Brave' (exploring determined discipleship from the book of James) was having a huge impact on the Spring Harvest family, and we were settling down to hear another message. The diminutive figure of Hae Woo made her way unassumingly onto the stage. She was being interviewed by our friends from Open Doors, Eddie Lyle and Emma Worrall. Nothing in our ministry up to this point had quite prepared us for the challenge that was about to come from the mouth of this heroine of the faith.

Hae Woo is from North Korea. She had been incarcerated for her faith in a labour camp, and is one of the bravest and most sold out Christians we have ever met. The power of her words was not lost in translation, and as she explained about starving in North Korea and all that it meant to be a Christian there, even the hardest of hearts in the room couldn't avoid being deeply moved. As Hae Woo explained what it looked like to plant a church in the labour camp where she was incarcerated, the true cost of following Jesus in her context seemed strikingly real. The church had to be planted in the toilets as this was the only place one could ever realistically gather in a queue. The gathered congregation would quietly whisper the truths of God together, knowing their very lives depended on not getting caught.

The church in the labour camp especially loved it when it would rain. This provided the only real opportunity to worship in song without fear of being caught. As the rain lashed down, the Christians would cry out in worship with the kind of unbridled freedom that they were denied the rest of the time. The interview with Hae Woo lasted about forty-five minutes, but the time flew by. You could hear a pin drop as the whole crowd of thousands hung on this incredible woman's words. As she drew to a close, she rose to her feet and, in what was little more than a whisper, sang 'Amazing Grace' in her native tongue. There was not a dry eye in the house as we all realised quite how different it would be to live out our faith were we to live instead in her homeland. This small North Korean woman instantly became a spiritual hero to the gathered crowd of thousands of western Christians.

The whole thing got us thinking: What does it really mean to be the church? Have we been blunted in this country? How would we respond if such persecution came our way? Do we really need that in order to live fully as the church in the UK? What might it look like for the church in our nation to be unleashed?

Jesus and His Youth Group

There is something about Jesus that makes people instinctively follow him. As he called the first disciples, he started a movement that went on to transform the world. Jesus' twelve disciples were certainly young, almost all under the age of eighteen and some even as young as fifteen. Their ages are not stated in Scripture so we need to look at what the Bible says, as well as gain a greater understanding of their cultural landscape. In the time of Jesus, a Jewish man married after the age of eighteen. Peter is the only one known to have been married. In Matthew 8:14-15, we learn that Peter had a wife when Jesus healed his mother-in-law.[1] For the rest of them to be unmarried, it's fairly clear they were teenagers. Jesus was thirty, and so his disciples would have been a generation younger, naturally respecting and following him as their Rabbi.

It's amazing that when the Lord wanted to change the world, he didn't start with a board of elders or a council of reference, but with a youth group. It's unlikely that the disciples fully understood what being part of this group would mean, but they chose to unite around Jesus and his cause. In John 1, we read how the disciples caught a glimpse of Jesus and dropped everything to follow him and do what he was doing. There was no guarantee of success. In fact, there wasn't even a guarantee that they were going anywhere specific. They would have had no idea how much following Jesus would transform their lives.[2] But they were still willing to risk everything they had to follow him. They truly were unleashed!

The first thing the disciples did was to find other people and involve them in following Jesus. Andrew found Simon Peter

(John 1:41-42). Philip found Nathaniel (John 1:45-46). Excited about following Jesus and his purposes, they couldn't help but invite people around them to be a part of it.[3] This also highlights the wonderful truth that Christianity is never solitary. It's a body that must always be serving together and adding to its number. It's the family we are a part of, and we are delighted to continue the work.

We often feel a little sorry for the disciples. They had a hard time and messed things up fairly often. We have sympathy, as our years in youth work showed us the highs and lows of working with teenagers. How challenging it is for the disciples that these years are recorded in the most-read book in the history of the world! It's remarkable that the church we will be looking at in the book of Acts is birthed amongst young people who were passed the baton at the Great Commission (Matthew 28) to continue to be disciples while also becoming disciple-makers themselves. They were unleashed to start the church in the face of much challenge and opposition. This bunch of young people is a wonderful example to us. Younger people are not always as out there as these disciples were, and many older people have amazingly adventurous spirits. Our prayer is that we might all, like the disciples, find a spirit of adventure and desire to follow Jesus wherever he leads, whatever our age.

What About Us?

In our day, we have an opportunity to play our part in being the church, in our context. Maybe it's time we reconnected with what the church was supposed to be in the first place. The American pastor Francis Chan puts it this way in his hugely popular book *Crazy Love*: 'I get nervous when I think of how we've missed who we are supposed to be, and sad when I think about how we're missing out on all that God wants for the people He loved enough to die for.'[4] Let's not allow ourselves to miss what it's all about. What started as a youth group is now the largest religion in the world and is growing rapidly.

Here in the UK, Christians are making a huge impact through ministries such as Christians Against Poverty, food banks, and Street Pastors and Angels. The church runs the majority of toddler groups, much of the nation's youth work, and remains pivotal on the ground. Yet there is still more.

Every one of us has an opportunity to be part of an unleashed church. Standing on the shoulders of the many giants that have come before us, we could see something amazing happen in our land. The church is wonderful, we love it, and are active and committed members within it; both of us take our roles as ordained church ministers seriously in seeing the nation impacted. There are so many possibilities in front of us, and it's a genuine privilege for all of us to have the opportunity to be in active service to the Saviour of the World.

In the Sermon on the Mount we are called as a body of Christians to be salt and light within the world, and then, 'a city on a hill that can't be hidden' (Matthew 5:13–14), yet so often we are tempted to hide ourselves from the world. The famous theologian Dietrich Bonhoeffer wrote about what it truly means to be the salt of the earth:

> Up to now we must have had the impression that the blessed ones were too good for this world, and only fit to live in heaven. But now Jesus calls them the salt of the earth—salt, the most indispensable necessity of life. The disciples, that is to say, are the highest good, the supreme value which the earth possesses, for without them it cannot live.[5]

As the people of God, we must be this salt. We are not too good for the world; we are the seasoning for it. We are hopeless people who've found great hope in Jesus, and those currently outside of Christ need this hope too. We must be out in the world, as without us it cannot live. What a challenge, but also what an opportunity.

As salt and light we also need to have a balanced approach to Word and Spirit. It can be so easy to emphasise one at the expense of the other, but an unleashed church must step forward with both in perfect harmony. The American Bible teacher R. T. Kendall famously puts it this way:

> If we have the Word without the Spirit, we tend to "dry up"; if we have the Spirit without the Word, we tend to "blow up"; if we have both Spirit and Word, we tend to "grow up" and "fire up." But when each is properly joined in common union, there is explosive power to be had.[6]

It's this explosive power that we need as the church. The combination of utter devotion, commitment, and reverence for the Word alongside the freedom, empowerment, and opportunities that come from a Spirit-filled life is what we really require. Jesus told the early church not to attempt their dangerous mission until they were baptised in the Spirit. Bible teacher Phil Moore puts it this way, 'Whichever way you read the book of Acts, one constant fact should be clear: the church grew rapidly in its early years because the Holy Spirit empowered God's people.'[7]

Our culture is tired of having tried so many things and found them wanting. The last few years in the UK have been particularly challenging for our nation. We as the church have such an opportunity to stand out in this landscape. Times are very uncertain, and none of us are sure of the outcome, but we are certain of who holds the future and the ultimate end of the story. This gives us Christians an incredible opportunity to show those around us what it's like to face the same cultural challenges as they do, but to do so alongside the living God.

What will be different about us in these times of confusion because we have Jesus? How much are we prepared to testify to the hope we have in him regardless of how swiftly our cultural backdrop is changing? What an incredible opportunity to witness. What a chance to show a different way, and for the church to be united in our mission, as the nation seems increasingly divided. In short, we need to own Christ as king and fully participate in his kingdom. This will mean returning to the revelation of a twentieth-century prophetic spokesman, Malcolm Muggeridge, who discovered what so many have missed:

> So I came back to where I began, to that other King, one Jesus; to the Christian notion that man's efforts to make himself personally and collectively happy in earthly terms are doomed to failure. He must indeed, as Christ said, be born again, be as a new man or he's nothing. So at least I have concluded, having failed to find in the past experience, present dilemmas, and future expectations, any alternative proposition. As far as I am concerned, it is Christ or nothing.[8]

If we live for Christ then we can be unleashed to see the nation changed. What does this really mean? We see it this way—'unleashing' describes the release of what is being restrained—what is being held back is the power of God and the people of God. Right now, spiritual earthquakes are happening in the places where missionaries have gone to for the last 200+ years. But in the places missionaries have come from during those same two centuries, hardly a tremor can be felt.[9]

The big question is, how can we see this kind of change in our nation in our day?

Part 1

UNLEASHED POWER

Acts 2:1–21

Acts 2:1-19

The Holy Spirit Comes at Pentecost

When the day of Pentecost came, they were all together in one place. ²Suddenly a sound like the blowing of a violent wind came from heaven and filled the whole house where they were sitting. ³They saw what seemed to be tongues of fire that separated and came to rest on each of them. ⁴All of them were filled with the Holy Spirit and began to speak in other tongues as the Spirit enabled them.

⁵Now there were staying in Jerusalem God-fearing Jews from every nation under heaven. ⁶When they heard this sound, a crowd came together in bewilderment, because each one heard their own language being spoken. ⁷Utterly amazed, they asked: "Aren't all these who are speaking Galileans? ⁸Then how is it that each of us hears them in our native language?" ⁹Parthians, Medes and Elamites; residents of Mesopotamia, Judea and Cappadocia, Pontus and Asia, ¹⁰Phrygia and Pamphylia, Egypt and the parts of Libya near Cyrene; visitors from Rome ¹¹ (both Jews and converts to Judaism); Cretans and Arabs—we hear them declaring the wonders of God in our own tongues!" ¹²Amazed and perplexed, they asked one another, "What does this mean?"

¹³Some, however, made fun of them and said, "They have had too much wine."

Peter Addresses the Crowd

[14]Then Peter stood up with the Eleven, raised his voice and addressed the crowd: "Fellow Jews and all of you who live in Jerusalem, let me explain this to you; listen carefully to what I say. [15]These people are not drunk, as you suppose. It's only nine in the morning! [16]No, this is what was spoken by the prophet Joel:

> [17]"In the last days, God says,
>   I will pour out my Spirit on all people.
> Your sons and daughters will prophesy,
>   your young men will see visions,
>   your old men will dream dreams.
> [18]Even on my servants, both men and women,
>   I will pour out my Spirit in those days,
>   and they will prophesy.
> [19]I will show wonders in the heavens above
>   and signs on the earth below,
>   blood and fire and billows of smoke.
> [20]The sun will be turned to darkness
>   and the moon to blood
>   before the coming of the great and glorious day
>   of the Lord.
> [21]And everyone who calls
>   on the name of the Lord will be saved."

1

The Holy Spirit Comes

'The Spirit-filled life is not a special, deluxe edition of Christianity. It is part and parcel of the total plan of God for His people.'

A. W. Tozer

Back in October 2016, I, Anne, was out jogging. It was a very foggy, dark morning and as I went up hill into the mist, I suddenly felt rather uneasy. There was no one around; it was early, but I found myself feeling unusually anxious and vulnerable. As I increased my pace, I turned my feelings quickly into prayer: 'Lord, please draw near, and comfort and reassure me. I need you.' Instead of feeling a sense of calm come over me, I began to sense something that I hadn't known before: I believe it was the voice of the King. He began to talk to me about an army rising in the nation. It was not a couple of sentences but quite a long narrative chunk. When I eventually got home a few miles and hills later, I found that I was able to recall word for word what He had said (and anyone who knows me knows that is quite a feat with my memory.) Here is what I penned that day:

'My child, I am raising up an army.
I am not raising up an army that carry weapons of destruction, that hold in their hands clubs and knives. I am raising up an army whose weapons are my Word and Spirit.'
I saw a man sharpening swords and felt the Lord was saying: 'I am sharpening my people. I am sharpening the tools in their hands, so that the truth can cut deep into the hearts of many.'
I then saw a child's face and the light from a huge flaming torch came near and lit up her face. I felt the Lord say: 'My royal

priesthood and my holy nation are being set apart. I am setting their faces like flint to walk into the darkness.'
Then I saw a huge procession of people carrying these flaming torches through the night.
'Not by might, nor by power, but by my Spirit,' said the Lord.
I understood this to mean that by his Holy Spirit he will shine on those living in darkness.
'I am raising up an army.' He kept reiterating these words. 'I am', he said, 'I am an army prepared to lay down the ways of the world and follow the way of the Spirit.'

Please do test these words as you would any word that someone shares with you. The words above have not left my heart and mind, and in fact, the Lord has kept adding weight to them together with other words that we will share throughout the book. We do believe that God is stirring in the nation at this time and that he is shaking us up in order to get the church's attention. We cannot put times or dates on the Lord's return or on the revival that we long to see, but what we are certain of is that the presence of the Lord is tangible and he is mighty to save. All across the land we have witnessed a growing hunger for Jesus from the saved and the lost. People are more desperate for Christ—for purpose, for answers, and for his kingdom to come.

As we join these people on a quest for more of the Lord, keen to be part of his Word and Spirit army that he is raising, we have been asking, 'Jesus, what do you want us to do? What are you speaking to us through your Word, through others, and how should we respond?'

That's why we turn to Acts. The early church were an army who set their faces like flint to walk into the darkness. The apostles shone with the power of the Holy Spirit and infected their area with the love of God in a life-transforming way. What can we take from their journey and implement right now in our context?

We believe that an undeniably important aspect of what we see in Acts is the work of the Holy Spirit. For the church to be unleashed and be all the Lord intends for us to be, we have to have the Spirit. The founding leader of the Vineyard movement, John Wimber, helpfully said this: 'The Holy Spirit holds the key to power encounters. Our openness and availability to His direction and enabling, anointing, and power is the catalyst for fulfilling the Great Commission.'[1] Wimber would talk about the Holy Spirit being removed from churches and 95 percent of 'ministry' continuing. Isn't that terrifying? Surely it's not okay that we could remove the work of the Spirit in our local churches and still largely continue as normal. Can you imagine the Acts church without the Holy Spirit's arrival at Pentecost? What would the narrative look like without his work? For a start, there would not have been the rapid spread of the Gospel, nor the multitudes of lives healed, restored, and transformed. In reality, the church would have quickly died out as the fear and persecution would have halted them in their tracks. The power of God raised Jesus from the dead and is still living and active today. That same power lives in us. There is so much more that he wants us to grasp.

We love the fact that the book of Acts is called 'Acts.' It is not called 'Facts'; it is not named after Luke or Paul. It is about the acts of the apostles as they begin to live out the Greatest Commandment and Commission of Christ. It is Acts, not facts (although we believe it to be true)—not just a narrative that we are called to digest and reflect on, but one that the Lord, by the arrival of the Holy Spirit at Pentecost, invites us all to participate in. We love the words of the theologian Tom Wright when he says, 'What we are reading, from this moment on, is the opening scene, or set of scenes, in a play whose action we ourselves are called to continue.'[2]

Let's look at those early chapters together. You might want to have Acts open next to you as you read *Unleashed* because the more Word you can combine with the Spirit, the better for transforming us all.

Setting the Scene

Luke writes predominantly to Gentile believers to confirm the gospel message and to share all that Jesus is doing through the apostles in the power of his Holy Spirit. This is his second book, having already authored Luke's Gospel, and it can often help to read them one after the other. Luke wants to remind us first and foremost that Jesus is the Resurrected Lord, who ascended into heaven, and who is about to send his Holy Spirit on the believers (Acts 1:1-11). Tom Wright reminds us: 'Luke desperately wants us to realize the importance of the Holy Spirit. Instead of being plunged into water (as John the Baptist demonstrated), you'll now be plunged into the Holy Spirit—this is for everyone.'[3]

The beginning of Acts speaks of a time when things were a bit complicated: the majority of believers were Jews, but as Gentiles became Christians, there was a struggle to work out how Jews and Gentiles could both be the people of God. Luke is keen to stress and affirm that Jesus is indeed the Messiah—the fulfilment of the Old Testament prophecies to Israel—and that is why salvation is spreading powerfully and effectively. Despite increasing opposition, the message of Jesus, by the power of the Spirit, keeps advancing because, as far as Luke is concerned, it is the sovereign plan of God.[4]

Before Jesus ascends into heaven, he tells the believers to wait in Jerusalem 'For the gift my Father promised, which you have heard me speak about. For John baptized with water but in a few days you will be baptized with the Holy Spirit' (Acts 1:4-5). Essentially Jesus is saying 'Don't do anything yet, it's pointless. You need to wait for the Spirit before you move.' The Bible teacher, the late John Stott, highlights how vital the Spirit is for the entire mission of the church: 'Without the Holy Spirit, Christian Discipleship would be inconceivable, even impossible. There can be no life without the life-giver, no understanding without the Spirit of Truth, no fellowship without the unity of the Spirit, no Christlikeness of character apart from His fruit, and no effective witness without His power. As a body without breath is a corpse, so the church without the Spirit is dead.'[5]

This realization and powerful moment in Scripture has to be enough to halt us in our tracks on every level: how much of our activity and decisions involve us waiting for the Spirit? How often are we expecting him to be a part of our day-to-day movements? What is stopping us from doing this?

To Our Knees

The apostles must have been consumed with grief. Their best friend, Saviour, and King had gone up into heaven (Acts 1:9), and there they are left alone wondering what on earth to do. The fear that they must have felt and uncertainty over the future would have been extreme. What's interesting is how they choose to respond: they all gather together constantly in prayer (Acts 1:14). Instead of stressing and worrying, they press in with prayer, not on their own but together.

A great book is *Fresh Wind, Fresh Fire* by Jim Cymbala of the Brooklyn Tabernacle in the USA. In the early part of the book, reveals that he felt called to take up a church of fewer than twenty people and recounts the deeply challenging early days of serving and not knowing what to do. In his desperation during one of his talks in a service, he ends up weeping and cannot go on. Cymbala says, 'I leaned into the pulpit, my face planted in my hands, and sobbed. Things were quiet at first, but soon the Spirit of God came down upon us. People began to call upon the Lord, their words motivated by a stirring within. "God help us," we prayed.'[6] In Cymbala's desperation, weakness, and vulnerability, God met with his people. Why? Because they turned to him. One of our biggest problems can be thinking that we know better than he does. The best starting point for any believer, or group of believers, is to be on their faces before the Almighty, seeking his face.

The early church was birthed in this place. It wasn't a strong army of people with all the answers, but a young band of folk who were more hungry and desperate for God than for anything else. And most importantly, they knew they were nothing and could do nothing without him.

The Arrival

We want to start here in the second chapter of Acts. This chapter frames the whole of the book that follows. The Sri Lankan church leader, Ajith Fernando, puts it this way: 'The second chapter of Acts introduces three of the most important keys to the entire book: the fullness of the Spirit (v. 1-13), the evangelistic ministry of the church (v. 14-41), and the community life of the believers.'[7] It's here in Acts 2 that our adventure really begins. For Luke, this is the start of things—with the Spirit coming at Pentecost, birthing the church, and giving it the power required to fulfil its appointed mission.[8]

The Spirit's arrival took place not just on any old day—it was specifically chosen and ordained by God to be the Day of Pentecost. This day was set apart as a Jewish harvest festival to celebrate the grain harvest, and took place fifty days after Passover (when harvesting traditionally began). The Lord was not just bringing in a material harvest but a spiritual one too. Three thousand souls were added to their number that day—'The first fruits of the Christian mission' (Acts 2:41)[9]—and it was only the beginning. Until Jesus returns, the time for sowing and reaping continues by the power of his Spirit. The fundamental need for the Spirit is not to be underestimated. Theologian James Montgomery Boice puts it this way: 'The disciples were being sent into the world with the Gospel. But they were not to go in their own strength. If they had, nothing would have happened.'[10]

The Holy Spirit comes down at Pentecost (Acts 2). The Counsellor, Convictor, truth teller: the One who would bring glory to Jesus by taking from what is His and making it known to us (John 16:5-16). The key to us knowing God more was released powerfully upon his children: 'Suddenly a sound like the blowing of a violent wind came from heaven and filled the whole house where they were sitting. They saw what seemed to be tongues of fire that separated and came to rest on each of them. All of them were filled with the Holy Spirit and began to speak in other tongues as the Spirit enabled them' (Acts 2:2-4). Wow! The Spirit fills the space and then fills the apostles. This is not just an outward experience, but an inward one too. It is also something that they hear and they see, and it didn't just happen to a couple of them in the room, it happened to every single one of them sitting there. When the wind comes, we witness what Jesus had been explaining to Nicodemus: 'The wind blows wherever it pleases. You hear its sound, but you cannot tell where it comes from or where it is going. So it is with everyone born of the Spirit' (John 3:8). We see the fire fall again like in Solomon's temple but also like the burning bush witnessed by Moses in Exodus (3:2). Fire falls on sacrifice (as with Elijah on Carmel; 1 Kings 19), but it also reveals the mighty presence of the Lord of all Lords.

This power that comes visibly and audibly is not dependent on status or position, but devotion to King Jesus. This same Spirit is at work right down through history and available to you and to us, right here and now. When we gather together and press in to seek him, he will come. When the Spirit does come, it is absolutely incredible. F. F. Bruce sums it up wonderfully saying that whatever we may say about Pentecost, one thing remains certain and really matters, 'the Spirit of God came upon them in power.'[11] The hugely encouraging thing is that this same power is available to all of us today. Whatever our background, God invites us to keep coming to be filled, and refilled, with his promised Holy Spirit.[12]

Here and Now

It is very difficult to pin down the entire nature of the Spirit of the Living God, but it is helpful to highlight examples of the Spirit at work. The narrative in Acts 2 reveals to us that the Holy Spirit can fall spontaneously and powerfully on the people, as we also see in

Acts 10:44: 'While Peter was still speaking these words, the Holy Spirit came on all who heard the message.' However, as the founder of the New Wine summer conference, David Pytches, points out, there are also times when the disciples prayed for the Holy Spirit, such as Acts 4:31: 'After they had prayed, the place where they were meeting was shaken. And they were all filled with the Holy Spirit and spoke the word of God boldly.'[13]

Sometimes when we have gathered in large groups, we have also, like the disciples, invited the Holy Spirit to come and move amongst us all. We have imagined the day of Pentecost and asked the Lord to do more of that, not for a mighty, smiley bless up, but so that we can be transformed and empowered for service. It is not that we haven't received the Holy Spirit at conversion, it is that the Lord longs to keep filling us afresh.

The danger, though, is when we assume that everyone's experience of the Spirit should (or will be) the same as ours, and we end up creating a system, process, or methodology by which being filled with the Spirit comes about. There is no magic formula, just the reality that God wants to empower his people for his mission.

Clive Calver (Gav's dad) helpfully outlines our confusion over baptism in the Holy Spirit: 'In the New Testament, the term "baptism in the Holy Spirit" is often associated with repentance and faith as part of the conversion experience. Since then, many Christians who have come into a deeper experience of the Holy Spirit" after conversion have referred to it as "a baptism of the Holy Spirit".'[14] Our Lord wants to enable his people to be bold, to know his power at work in and through our lives, to release gifts of the Spirit upon us so that other people's lives can be impacted and transformed. How he does that is up to him, and it cannot be confined in a box or named as a formula.

One of our most prominent memories was when we were running the youth programme at the New Wine summer conference. Everyone was worshipping and lifting their hands to the music, completely sold out in praise. The atmosphere in the room was electric, the Presence of God palpable. As we continued to get lost in wonder and adoration before our King there began to be a small commotion in the middle of the crowd. Eventually, it began to feel like a distraction so we carefully drew a couple of the chattering individuals out to the back of the venue. Filled with joy and excitement, they began to explain what had just miraculously happened to their friend. She had self-tattooed the word 'worthless' on her forearm with a pen knife and been going through agony over how she viewed herself. As we were mid-worship, proclaiming who our Lord is, celebrating how he saw us and receiving his love and power into our hearts and lives, something incredible ensued: her arm was completely healed. No one prayed or moved or made it happen. The Lord just touched her and erased not only the word, but also the scarring right down her arm. Her friends were literally leaping and jumping and praising God!

Our God is desperate to encounter his children by the power of the Spirit, not just over 2,000 years ago, but here and now too. He is interested in every one of us, not just the loudest. The Bishop of Berwick, Mark Tanner, has written about some of the struggle in this area being himself more introverted: 'For many of us, especially those who are more introvert in personality, this means that we are in an uncomfortable place where charismatic culture can seem shallow, loud, driven and insensitive, but where we love the stuff that God is doing.'[15] We must make sure that we do not make things too narrow in their focus and exclude others in the process. The Holy Spirit is not limited to working through any particular personality type.

The question is, are we waiting for him? Seeking him? Longing for more? Expecting him to move? Are we even in a place of believing fire can fall and wind can blow?

Seek His Face

There was a young guy who was planning on setting up a shelter for the homeless because he had a passion to help them. He and his friends looked online for space they could rent in the city so that they could invite those in need into a warm environment for a cup of coffee or tea. Eventually, they found what they believed was a suitable space, got set up, and opened the doors, hopeful and waiting expectantly for the homeless to come. A year later they were still waiting—no longer feeling expectant, but rather hopeless and doubting themselves and their decision to open the shelter. At the brink of giving up and closing the space down, they got to their knees in desperation and began to pray, asking God to help them, to show them what to do, to come by the power of his Holy Spirit. Later that day, they wandered out onto the street and down to the corner, where they encountered a man living rough and alone. They began to talk to him and their longed-for ministry began.

Hearing this story we were so challenged and sympathetic towards these guys. How easy it is to have a vision, dream, or idea and then to set about making it happen our own way! All that time, work, and energy, and the Lord was just waiting for them to seek his face. The Lord Almighty wanted to birth this ministry and lead it his way—that way they would see lives transformed. It is interesting that at the point of nearly giving up, not knowing what to do next, that is when we see great breakthrough happen, but it comes from a place of prayer. God has an agenda that he calls us to join in with, and he longs for us to ask him about what that looks like from just where we are.

The last words Jesus speaks before he ascends into heaven are: 'But you will receive power when the Holy Spirit comes upon you; and you will be my witnesses in Jerusalem, and in all Judea and Samaria, and to the ends of the earth' (Acts 1:8). Then Jesus is taken up before their eyes (1:9). Why would he make these words his last? Perhaps because it was so important for the believers to hear them and take them seriously. Maybe because in order for the gospel to go right out to the four corners of the earth, the Holy Spirit was absolutely vital–it was not something they could tackle alone. It's interesting that they return to Jerusalem (1:12), the first place on the list that Jesus calls them to witness. The apostles' thoughts could easily remain on the Lord ascending to heaven, but instead they head to where they are called to go and begin to press in with prayer. One commentator observes: 'Instead of indulging in wishful thinking or apocalyptic speculation, the disciples must accomplish their task of being witnesses to Jesus. The scope of their task is worldwide. It begins with Jerusalem, Judea, and Samaria, and it stretches to the end of the earth.'[16]

And so it began back then, over 2,000 years ago, and the mandate still remains today. The question is, where is our Jerusalem? Are we headed there? Are we watching and waiting and praying? Are we aware of the Spirit's empowering and being witnesses in the places he has called us to be? Our fear is that we will just get on with our own life plan and not fully join in with the saints that have gone before, taking his gospel to the nations.

Luke quickly draws us to the Holy Spirit and emphasises that Luke will move when we begin to pray. He is the Almighty trigger to launch inspired, world-changing initiatives. The Spirit births confidence and vision; he releases the captives and equips the saints. All that flows out of the early chapters in Acts is because of the power of the Holy Spirit and nothing else.

YES, but How?

For you:

- As Christians we are filled with the Holy Spirit at conversion. However, would you like a fresh empowering of the Holy Spirit? In what areas do you feel like you are operating out of your own strength? Why not ask a couple of committed Christians to pray for you?
- Could it be time to commit your work to the Lord again, asking his Holy Spirit to be the empowerer of your every day?
- Are you sensitive to the Holy Spirit's leading in the ministries you are involved with (at home, in the work place, on the street, at church)?

For a group:

- Do you sense that there is an army rising in the UK? Why? What are you seeing?
- Is the Holy Spirit the glorious trigger-launcher of what is happening in your area, through your church/ministry/work?
- If not, how can he be more involved in what you are doing?
- The disciples waited in prayer for their sense of direction. When did you last spend time waiting for his leading? What happened?

Further Reading:

A.W. Tozer, *Alive in the Spirit* (Bloomington: Bethany House Publishers, 2016)

J. Wimber, *Power Evangelism* (London: Hodder & Stoughton, 2013)

R.T. Kendall, *Holy Fire* (Lake Mary: Charisma House, 2014)

M. Tanner, *The Introvert Charismatic* (Oxford: Monarch Books, 2015)

2

Time for Act 2

'Champions are made from something they have deep inside of them—a desire, a dream, a vison.'

Muhammad Ali

Imagine yourself in the room with the apostles in the early part of Acts. You are huddled together feeling anxious, not knowing what is going to happen next. Wondering if you will be hunted down and killed for following the King of the Jews. Can you put your faith in these others with you? Will they work out a way ahead? You ponder these questions in your mind, and they begin to be added to: Jesus did say to wait here in Jerusalem, right? But I wonder why? What's this Holy Spirit, this gift, going to look like, and will it really make a difference to what happens from here? After all, without Jesus, we are truly sheep without a shepherd. He may have risen and ascended, but we can't do that; we will just die. Those few days in the city, pressing in with prayer must have felt like forever.

Transformation

What strikes us reading Acts 1 and 2 again is the totally remarkable shift between the believers we meet before the Holy Spirit descends and the ones we witness afterwards. Phil Moore notes: 'It must have been frustrating to be part of God's people before the great party of Pentecost.'[1] In those moments when the fire falls and fills and enables, the people are transformed. And all of a sudden, they move. Before this, they are all together, probably filled with fear. After it, they all step out, clearly consumed with faith. 'Consider this:

17

2 Chronicles 7—when the temple was dedicated—was not the only time fire fell from heaven onto the temple. It also happened in Acts 2 when the church was born. The disciples were united and praying when tongues of fire fell on them. They were the temple. Fire fell on them. And you know the rest of the story.'[2]

Fire falls and lives are changed forever. Take Peter for example. Immediately, he stands up and addresses the crowd. Where does that confidence appear from? The Holy Spirit. Otherwise he would have done it sooner. Filled with fire, anointed words proclaiming who Jesus is and what he has done spill forth from his mouth, dramatically affecting the listeners. But Peter is so normal and ordinary and has made so many mistakes, yet is transformed by the power of the Spirit. This gives us all great hope.

Let's take a closer look at Peter's track record. I, Gavin, had the privilege of sharing a platform a few years ago on a Care for the Family tour with the amazing communicator Rob Parsons. It was so brilliant to see him speak, and to learn and develop as a communicator myself by watching such a person in action close-up. During this tour, Rob spent a lot of time talking about the disciple Peter in a fascinating way. He would often joke about what Peter's school report might have looked like:

Dear Mr. and Mrs. Fisher (the fictional name Rob gave to Peter's parents),

Sadly, the master had to tell your son to get behind him as he made a silly comment. Your son ruined the ascension with another silly comment. Peter nearly drowned whilst trying to walk on water in PE, and worst of all, he cut someone's ear off in the garden this evening! Peter was hardly the man on whom common sense would say you would trust to lead your church.

For so many people, their favourite Bible character is, in fact, Peter. Not the seemingly all-conquering Paul, but Peter. Rob writes elsewhere that he believes we love Peter so much because he reminds us of ourselves. He shows us there is hope beyond our failure, and that God so often uses the weak not the successful; he has a plan for us beyond our failures.[3] We are so much more than our previous mistakes. The world may seem to want to write us off so quickly, throw us on the scrap heap at the first opportunity, or write us off as 'not up to it'. Jesus is not like that. He's the God of the second, third, and thousandth chance. He doesn't want our history, our low self-image, the views of others, or anything else to restrict how he might choose to use us today.

Peter gives us great hope. If he can become the rock on which the church can be built (Matthew 16:18), then who knows what he might choose to do with one of us? Here was a man who was following Jesus right up to the point where he is brought into the room and questioned: 'You are not one of his disciples, are you?' says the girl at the door. Suddenly fear sets in. 'I am not,' he replies (John 18:17). Peter stays close by; he wants to be near his master, his saviour, but he goes on to deny Jesus two more times. The fear and anxiety that overtake Peter in this moment of time do not appear to have the same effect in Acts 2. In fact, we see a different man arise. The environment hadn't got any easier. It was still very dangerous to be followers of Jesus, but his fear is overtaken by faith.

Peter is now full of trust in the Son of God, and as the early chapters of Acts reveal, he did become the rock on which the church was built. It is Peter who preaches the first evangelistic sermon, but only as a representative of the Twelve. His role as the rock is always as a part of a community, never just as an individual.[4] That's why we, too, must work as part of a body, not as maverick individuals.

What's also amazing is that no matter how incredible the things Peter saw and did were, he never got above his station. Nowhere in the New Testament are we told that Peter or his successors had any special position or privilege in the church. Certainly Peter in his two letters claimed to be nothing more than an apostle (1 Peter 1:1), an elder (1 Peter 5:1), and a servant of Jesus Christ (2 Peter 1.1).[5] We need to be unleashed into all we can be, but we must never forget who the King is and that our role is simply to serve him.

Just like for Peter, when the Spirit of God impacts his people today, we are no longer the same and we cannot sit still. This is so deeply challenging. We need to allow the Lord to transform us and give us another chance. The story of Peter shows so clearly that our King is the God of the second chance, or indeed the hundredth chance, if like us, you need that many.

If you think for a few minutes about your church as you know it, is it more like the huddled, fearful, questioning crew, or is it like the unstoppable, faith-filled, bold believers who scatter to share the good news? We don't know what you are going to say to that—our longing is a 'yes' to the second part of the sentence, but if you have known church as we have experienced it, many of us have a long way to go.

The simple truth is that until we do what they do in Acts 1, we do not believe we will have an Act 2 in the life of the church. And until we experience Act 2, no other mighty Acts can follow that will transform the church upside down and back-to-front. This isn't a one-time thing either—God is seeking out children who are not just looking to their leaders to do this, but beginning to press in themselves, over and over again. We are one family, and Jesus wants to use every single part of his body to change the world.

Supernatural Equipping

Peter stands up, raises his voice, and speaks to the crowd: fuelled by the Spirit of God, he has revelation in that very moment to express what is happening. He begins to declare the words of the prophet Joel, with deep conviction, are manifesting—that they are witnessing the outpouring right there: 'In the last days, God says, I will pour out my Spirit on all people [not just prophets, priests, and kings]. Your sons and your daughters will prophesy, your young men will see visions, your old men will dream dreams. Even on my servants both men and women, I will pour out my Spirit in those days and they will prophesy (Acts 2:17-18).' And it goes on.

Almost as soon as the 'experience' of Pentecost has happened (although the effects will last forever), Peter takes us straight into Scripture to highlight the significance of what just occurred. His audience would be familiar with the writing of Joel, and Peter knew that the words, combined with powerful manifestations, would enable those watching to attempt to make sense of what was happening. For Peter, he had in front of him those who not long before had been so hostile to Jesus. One theologian puts it this way: 'Seeing before him the very crowd of Passion Week, those whose voices had cried "Hosanna . . . Barabbas . . . Crucify," Peter turns to the central truth of the Gospel.'[6]

The crowd were familiar with the ancient texts and were constantly looking for answers to the world that they found themselves living in. Peter was putting 'meat on the bones' of their thinking. Tom Wright notes: 'What Peter was offering wasn't simply an explanation for strange behaviour, even for strange religious phenomena (always a dangerous thing in a crowded city at the time of a big religious and national festival). It was a challenge: we've arrived! The journey is over! Here are the signs of the destination! Time to have a fresh look around and see where we are.'[7]

Old men with dreams, young men with visions—yes, please Lord, more! Prophetic words, signs, and wonders—we long for all of it, not just in the building, but during our working week. The key is the encounter because it is this moment that then triggers the whole narrative of Acts. Don't hear us wrong, we need to continue encountering the power of the Spirit and hearing the voice of God, but if it doesn't happen at all, then very little changes in our lives. This can leave us not living fully in the power of the Spirit.

This powerful equipping of the Spirit was not just for that moment, but also to unleash the church into supernatural gifts and a world-changing mission today, and until the Lord returns.

Daniel 10

About a year ago, I, Anne, was listening to twins in their 70s talking about revival coming to the UK. They were so excited to come over from Israel to Britain because they believe that something incredible is going to happen here. One of them began to talk about the fire of God that will rise throughout every corner and area of the British Isles, and then will move out like arrows into Europe and the Americas. As she shared about the fire filling the land, I began to feel really weak and wobbly, slightly sick, and then my breathing began to go shallow. My instant thought was that I was falling ill or perhaps had some deeper problem. In order not to make a scene, I stood up from my seat and tried to head towards the door. I thought I could compose myself better out of the room. However, before I reached the doorway, my legs gave way and I fell face down onto the carpet. It was the strangest experience.

All of a sudden, I became very aware of the awesome power of God and suddenly certain of my own frailty. I knew that in one second, the breath could be snatched from my body—such was the might of my King. This has been my first and only realisation of what the Fear of the Lord really looks like.

The conversation in the room was continuing because the few people sitting there were fascinated by the vision the twins had shared. I knew they were talking, but it did not feel like I was in the same room as they were. I heard in the distance the other twin say, regarding my sudden display by the door, 'Is she for real?' and my friend's reply, 'Yes, don't worry. She is okay.' Please be assured this kind of behaviour has never happened to me before!

Eventually, I was able to move (I was becoming a bit concerned about making it in time for the school run), and I slowly got to my feet and travelled home, wondering what on earth that encounter was for. It felt like the glory of the Lord had been all around me.

Later that day, the prophetic twins were at our church sharing again and praying for people. I decided to sit near the back and read my Bible—I think I had enough for one day. The Lord drew me very quickly to Daniel, chapter 10 (a chunk of scripture I was not greatly familiar with) and began to highlight words to me on the page:

Daniel has a vision and it says 'I had no strength left, my face turned deathly pale and I was helpless (10:8b).' It goes on: 'A hand touched me and sent me trembling to my hands and knees' (10:10), 'I bowed with my face to the ground' (10:15), and then 'My strength is gone; I can hardly breathe' (10:17). The words were such an encouragement regarding my behaviour earlier that day, and I simply felt the Lord explaining that I had not had the vision, but I had had the response to the vision. I was left thinking, 'Goodness me, how did Daniel cope with both? Or how did Isaiah for that matter?'

We hope this doesn't sound too crazy to you. This is not our normal every day, but experiences like these has been key in forming our thoughts for writing this book. Why? You may ask. Because if there is a mighty move of the Spirit coming in our lifetime, which we hope and pray that there is, then these encounters are key triggers for creating an urgency in our spirit and a desperation to crack on with his work.

You see, the Daniel 10 revival encounter was not the same as the Acts 2 one that fell on the disciples, but it achieved a similar thing: God was doing something supernatural to awaken the children of God, to anoint and equip them for a life's work that was like nothing they had been part of before. He was not just doing it then; he is also doing it now. This story is just one of many.

What Now?

As ministers of the gospel, we feel so challenged by these first two chapters in Acts and how we take the whole church from believing that attending a Sunday service is not what makes us Christians, nor is singing or listening well during it. How do we equip the whole church to long for transformation in their own lives and in the lives of the lost?

We know you will have heard it before, but church was never meant to be a building anyway. It's the people that make up the body of Christ. Years and years and years of 'doing church' has taken up such a deep root in our western world view, we need a major move of God to transform us now and going forward into the future. Don't hear us wrong, Jesus loves us meeting together and worshiping and pressing in to seek him, but he longs to reveal so much more.

We sometimes wonder if Jesus were returning for his bride now, how would he react? What would he be looking for? Would he grieve over our consumer mentality, our lethargy, and our distorted view of what being a Christian means? We believe he would rejoice over the multiplication in prayer meetings happening all over the UK, the ministries that share the gospel as well as help the broken, the churches supporting those who scatter into their work places, sharing Christ in the darkness.

Living 'All Out'

The early Christians knew that they might die for their faith. When they received the gospel and were baptized in the Holy Spirit, it was with the understanding that martyrdom could be the end of their story—and yet they still chose to follow. Emperor Nero, taking up the reins of power (probably by the end of the Acts story), was burning Christians as candles in his garden. These believers were giving their whole life to Christ, no matter what the cost, and counting persecution as a privilege.

Something happened in their lives that was so significant when they accepted Christ that they could take no other view and live no other way but by advancing the gospel to the nations. We believe the answer lies in the power of the Spirit to transform our lives, even now in our Western world, and the discovery of, as we begin to encounter not just a building but the master builder, Jesus. When his love consumes us, we realize what he has done for us, and we cannot help but feel compelled to spread his story.

If we genuinely struggle with a desire to share the Good News of Jesus with others, perhaps we need to go back to our upstairs rooms and seek him again, afresh. We would suggest there is more of himself that he longs to reveal to you, and more of his Holy Spirit that he longs to pour out into your life. As we write, we are conscious of those who have sought to share their story with the lost, to stand out in their culture and yet feel quite disillusioned. Jesus always removed himself to solitary places before he continued to minister; maybe he just wants you to come away with him and be refreshed and restored again.

Moving Outwards

Interestingly, we have been occupying a different space recently. We have felt continually urged and nudged to take our faith further from the building. It is scary. Taking prayer ministry into the public space can set us up for strange looks and accusation, but that was a constant reality for the early believers, and Jesus told us to expect it.

The power that the believers experience is not something that keeps them in the building, but compels them out onto the streets. They don't stay stuck in the blessing, but are empowered to make disciples. We have to honestly say that when we are not preaching or leading (which is rare), we want the 'bless up.' The idea that encounters in the building drives us out to the lost is probably not the top of our priorities each Sunday.

Perhaps our whole view of church needs addressing. We write that nervously because there are so many incredible leaders seeking him first and longing for his will amongst his people. However, maybe it is time, bit by bit, to unpack why we do what we do and to ask if what we are walking in now is actually the plan of God for his church in our nation now. Because if it isn't, what is? And how do we journey towards that?

Alan Scott's book *Scattered Servants* is a challenging read for those longing for more of the Acts church today. He says, 'It's hard to reach a city when we stay in the building and when our ministry models revolve around expanding our services. Gathered environments grow churches; scattered servants reach cities.'[8] He does not suggest we never need to gather, but that we gather to then scatter. That meeting together is a necessity to keep scattering. As we keep seeking to pray, worship, read the Word, and be filled with the Spirit, fellowshipping together, it serves as fuel to enable us to fulfil the Great Commission of making disciples all over the world—wherever we find ourselves.

Have a Go

One morning, after praying and asking the Spirit to fill me afresh, I, Anne, headed off on the school run. Nearing the gate, I met my friend and asked her how she was doing. With our two boys nagging us to keep walking, she quickly told me that she was suffering with agonizing back pain. I did my usual 'So sorry to hear that. Can I do anything to help?' along with a genuine concerned face, but then I felt the nudge from the Lord: 'Offer to pray, Anne.' There I was wishing I hadn't asked him to fill me and give me opportunity that day, and trying to ignore it, I continued with my concerned questions, but I couldn't shake it. With a deep breath I said, 'Can I pray for you?' 'Yes, do that,' she responded immediately. 'Can I do it now?' 'Oh, okay,' came the reply. 'Is it okay if I put my hand on your back?' I tentatively inquired. 'Oh, okay,' she graciously responded. With two boys staring up at us and parents scattered around, I simply prayed that in the name of Jesus, her back would be healed. Peace came at once—flooding in so I didn't want to move. She felt it too. 'Thanks, Anne, that's very kind,' she stuttered as we made final steps to the gate.

The next morning she called across the playground to me: 'You are not going to believe it, Anne. My back feels so much better!' As joy and courage flooded my soul, I simply pointed my arm and finger towards heaven and said, 'Praise him!'

Not a big thing really in the scope of things, but this is, I suppose, Acts in action: the boldness from the Spirit of the Living God and the courage to step out and speak up. Our dream is that she comes to know Jesus, and that these reports are shared, prayed into, and advanced as we share them with 'the church'.

Yes, but How?

For you:

- Do you relate to the Peter of John's Gospel—the one who found it just a bit too tough to say he was a follower of Jesus when the truly challenging moment came?
- Have you had a situation where you wish you had spoken up for Jesus or declared that you did indeed 'know him'?
- Whatever has happened in the past does not have to define your future. Peter shows us that our Lord is the god of the second chance. Perhaps you might want to take a moment to ask the Lord to help you dust yourself down and start again.

For your group:

If this is relevant to you:

Francis Chan says: 'Take a deep breath. Lay all your stress at his feet. Explain to him your confusion regarding the difference you see between your church and the church you read about. Tell him your dissatisfaction with the lack of power in your life'.[9]

Spend a few moments praying and then just quietly waiting.

After a short time, see if anyone is sensing anything or feeling anything further.

Keep praying and pressing in. There is no rush.

Is there anything specific that he is asking you to do?

A lesson from the Acts church

In Acts 3, Peter is asked for money by a beggar. He has no money, but instead says in verse six: 'Silver or gold I do not have, but what I do have I give you. In the name of Jesus Christ of Nazareth, walk.' Sometimes we answer everyone's requests instead of considering that, like Peter, we may have a more significant counter-offer. Our power is not of this world.

Further Reading:

A. Scott, *Scattered Servants* (Colorado Springs: David C. Cook, 2018)

F. Chan, *Letters to the Church* (Colorado: David C Cook, 2018)

T. Virgo, *The Spirit-Filled Church* (Oxford: Lion Hudson, 2011)

3

Walking on Water

'You are braver than you believe, stronger than you seem, and smarter than you think.'

Winnie the Pooh

We can no longer claim to be young adults. Married with kids and having recently entered our forties, we have ticked off many of the rites of passage on offer and are now faced with the temptation of domestic bliss, settling into a rhythm of comfort and ease. Alternatively, maybe it's time for a mid-life crisis? Probably not; neither of us wants to ride a motorbike. We want to continue to be radical and open to all the Lord might have for us. Christians are movers, not settlers, who should write our addresses, jobs, and dreams in pencil, thus allowing the Lord to reshape them as he pleases.

Graduating from Bible College some twenty years ago, we were surrounded by many who wanted to change the world and go out on a limb to serve Jesus. Our early days in Youth for Christ were spent around those who were more interested in sharing the gospel than in negotiating terms and conditions. The faith that filled our bones was edgy, exciting, and worth giving everything for.

Fast forward to today, and I, Gavin, found myself meeting an old friend—the one who was such an encouragement to me in my early years of faith, spurring me on in my walk with Jesus. He knew what it was to have God in the centre of his life and would talk passionately about his love of the Lord. However, today's conversation was different. He was still speaking animatedly and enthusiastically, but it was not about Jesus. It was about his new patio.

I left the conversation with thoughts flooding through my mind.

What had happened in the last couple of decades to see godly, eternal passion transferred to concrete in gardens? Why do we keep bumping into Christians our age who are more evangelistic about their new kitchen than they are about Jesus? How is it that there is seemingly more inspiration for life on the pages of the Ikea catalogue than in the Bible? When did everything become so safe?

Many of our contemporaries seem consumed by home ownership, kids, school places, nice holidays, work/life balance, and physical fitness. There's nothing wrong with these things, but they are not the pinnacles of life. No, the true reason for our existence is spelt out by Jesus in John 10:10: 'I have come that you may have life, and have it to the full.' Is domestic bliss really living life to the full or is it a recipe that points towards a mid-life crisis?

We need to start extending our prophetic imaginations as to what is possible. We need a gear change in Christianity: a new perspective that remembers our identity in Christ and seeks to transform his world. The pastor Malcolm Macdonald puts it this way: 'We spend our lives seeking safety, ease and comfort. Yet, the church in the New Testament ran towards sacrifice, servanthood and risk. What is our goal in life: getting our needs met or laying our lives down?'[1] Is it time we refocused our priorities?

We both love the film *Amazing Grace*,[2] all about the abolition of the slave trade. We went to watch it together in the cinema when it first came out in 2006 whilst on holiday in America. The film shook us to the core as we saw the life of William Wilberforce unfold in front of our eyes on the big screen. You see him give everything he has for his cause, irrespective of what the world around him may think. He is often mocked and scorned, but Wilberforce gives everything, even his health, for the sake of his God-given cause. There is one particular moment within the film that stood out to us to hold onto. Wilberforce is best friends with William Pitt, who goes on to become the youngest ever UK prime minister in 1783 at the age of 24. He left office in 1801, but served as prime minister again from 1804 until his death in 1806. When Pitt is thinking of running for PM for the first time, he tells Wilberforce of his plan, who, in turn, basically says he is too young. Pitt replies along the lines of: 'I'm young enough to not yet realise that I can't change the world!' What a moment. It is young people who often spearhead change and revolutions because they are as yet unblemished by the cynicism of the world. Young people are eager and often envisage a greater future than many of us can imagine. Perhaps that is what the Lord wants from us when he tells us to come to him like children. Maybe we should be more hopeful and less worn down by the years. Perhaps it's time to dream again of a brighter future, a different world, a vibrant church at the heart of the nation.

As we left the cinema together, a pair of blissfully happy young people in our mid-twenties, we challenged one another to try and live the rest of our lives utterly sold out to the cause of Christ. To do all we could to spur one another on, to relentlessly pursue God and his kingdom and to not be tamed by the ageing process. This is not always easy, but something we are still seeking to do. To both remain unleashed in our service of the King.

Of course, we want a nice patio, but we would far rather be passionate about our faith. We want to be part of a church who choose Jesus first and to join him on the risky water instead of staying in the safety of the boat. After all, the disciples who stayed in the boat also made a choice. We always seem to assume that it's only Peter who chooses something in that moment. No, not doing anything, being apathetic, remaining safe—these are all choices too.

Time to Be Brave

We travel a lot, which is fun but also exhausting. One summer we were doing our usual crazy conference preaching all over the place and found ourselves at a particular conference. There was one specific meeting where neither of us had any responsibility for anything and could just sit there in the huge tent and receive. The preacher spoke powerfully and passionately about the need for the church to rise up in our day and be what the UK required. At the end of the talk the preacher gave a call for anyone feeling challenged about the need to be distinct for Christ in our secular landscape to make their way to the front.

I, Gavin, shot out of my seat and went forward. I don't often respond to talks as I'm usually giving them, and it's the height of preaching arrogance to respond to your own talk. I knew this call was for me, and as I went forward, it would not have mattered to me if no one else did. I stood at the front of this large tent, and I felt the Lord challenge me that I needed to be braver for him in this next chapter of life. I took a look around the tent, and seeing the thousands of other Christians there, foolishly felt that I was doing okay, comparatively speaking. I immediately felt chastised by the Lord and felt a strong sense that I needed to look upwards to him and not sideways at others.

I stood there at the front and felt myself facing up to the reality of what it might mean to be brave. What might it cost? Where might it take me? Who would hate me? How would I keep going? What would it mean for my family? As these thoughts flooded through my mind, I felt myself begin to weep. Not cry a little, really weep. The tears poured freely as I faced up to what the Lord might be calling me into. So often we assume that bravery involves no fear and is easy for some. It is not. It was the great man himself, Nelson Mandela, who said, 'I learned that courage was not the absence of fear, but the triumph over it. The brave man is not he who does not feel afraid, but he who conquers that fear.'³

We all have the option to conquer our fears or submit to them. Brave people are developed, not born. Bravery is about acting when we can; it's not just feelings. This is shown in Esther when she goes to see the king in the book of Esther, chapter four. She is given a chance to be brave and is prepared to be so, even going so far as to say that 'If I perish, I perish' (Esther 4:16). After a little persuasion, she promised to break the law and approach the king. In this moment Esther had now conquered her human fears and was prepared to put her very life on the line for her people. James E. Smith puts it this way in relation to Esther: 'Rashness acts without fear; bravery, in spite of it.'[4]

I wiped my face and went to tell Anne about this encounter. I told no one else.

On the last night of the summer holidays, we were sitting around, having a family meal. Once we had finished eating, we prayed for one another ahead of a return to normality after a fun summer together. At the end of our prayer times, we try to have some moments of silence to see if the Lord wants to say anything to us. We are desperate for our kids to learn that prayer is a conversation and not a monologue. After a minute or so in silence, our daughter Amelie spoke up, knowing nothing of my encounter at the front of that tent. A little tentatively she said, 'Dad, it's a bit weird, but I think Jesus wants you to be braver going forward.' Understandably, I was somewhat taken aback and prepared to hear what the Lord was saying loud and clear to me. However, we don't think it was just a message for one individual. We wholeheartedly believe that the Lord is calling his church here in the UK to be braver in this next season both inside and outside of the building.

We are living in a time when being a Christian is like being a cultural alien, a stranger in a foreign land and a part of a marginalised minority. In many ways we actually find ourselves in a 'pre-Christian' context. Many talk of the UK as a post-Christian nation, but we don't see it like this. It's not that generations have heard about Jesus and rejected this because they disagree. Many have never heard of him and, as such, 'pre-Christian' is the right perspective. In so many ways our context is very much like the context for the Acts church, just nowhere near as difficult. Nonetheless, we must not underestimate how much of an outsider you can be made to feel if you choose to follow Jesus. A husband wrote about this in the *Daily Telegraph,* describing how he pretended to his wife that he was going cycling each Sunday morning as it would be too much for her to accept that he was actually going to church. He would leave the house on his bike and in his Lycra, and instead of cycling a twenty-mile route would pull up at his local church for the service.

My wife and I have been married for 12 years, and have three children. We've never had a problem expressing our feelings to each other. We share the same politics, the same taste for Scandi noir and offbeat comedy boxsets, and the same contempt for personalised number plates. Why, then, do I find it so difficult to tell her the truth about where I'm really going every Sunday? It would probably be easier to admit frequenting a lap-dancing club or to confess to being a Trump admirer.[5]

So in this landscape where we are so unusual, it's important to be brave. We ourselves understand this only too well. There is no greater conversation stopper than telling anyone who has no faith what we do for a living. We have learned to be creative when we are inevitably asked what it is we do for a living.

As well as being brave, we must make sure that we are kind. Christians have a poor record when it comes to treating those around them who don't agree with them with the love and kindness they deserve. We must not be foolhardy in our bravery, but treat everyone with the dignity that they deserve and as someone that Jesus died for. I, Gavin, remember an early moment of Christian fundraising that I was involved in. I'd not long taken over leading Youth for Christ, and I headed to the city of London to meet a Christian banker. We had a great time and connected well, and his gift to the ministry that day was incredibly generous. I walked out of there feeling on top of the world, like my day had been amazing. I walked past a Tesco Express where a woman was crying in the doorway. I simply walked past.

As I passed the doorway I felt the Lord challenge me in the depths of my guts. How dare I make such an effort with the millionaire and yet walk past a woman in need? Feeling suitably chastised I went back and asked the lady if she was okay. She had been attacked by her boyfriend and had run away and needed to get to her mum's house, but she didn't have the money to get there. I hailed a black cab and asked how much to get to where she needed. '20 quid,' said the taxi driver. I looked in my wallet and that was all I had, so I gave it to him and waved the woman off.

As the taxi pulled away, I felt challenged by the whole experience. It is not okay to treat anyone more highly than anyone else. All people are made in the image of God and must all be treated with love. We need to be brave in this season, but we also need to be kind. The brave part is often easier than the kindness, but the two need to go together. The best example we can think of is when Joseph was intending to divorce Mary after finding out she was pregnant. Believing his betrothed had been unfaithful, he wanted to do the right thing and divorce her. However, he wanted to do it kindly, away from the crowds and with as much love as possible. Perhaps this is what it means to be brave and kind. Treating people the right way and loving them whilst not losing truth. Also, like Joseph, we want to be up for a complete change of direction in the light of an angelic visitation.

An Example of Dangerous Living

Our friend Sam Ward works at the Message Trust, and is a wonderful example of someone who is living out their faith bravely and encouraging others to do the same. Here is some of his story.

firenado [fahyer-ney-doh]
noun (pl. fire-na-does, fire-no dos)
a phenomenon created when turbulent air rapidly rises from the site of burning

I love Firenado day or Pentecost as some like to call it. Acts 2: it's a new day and the disciples gathered, united in purpose and proximity. A roar is heard from the direction of heaven. There's no mention of who was first to hear it, but within moments every ear hears that heavenly hurricane as it fills every square inch of the house. Seated, the disciples watch as the wind ignites into flame, divides, and then delicately descends to rest upon their heads. Sensory overload. They've never witnessed something like this before. They saw and they heard, but did they feel anything? Did the wind wobble them? Did the fire warm them? The Holy Spirit filled them, and the tongues of fire were soon replaced with new tongues that enabled the gospel to be proclaimed to the ears of all nations.

Exchange the Pentecost property from Acts 2 with a freezing cold conservatory in the suburbs of Manchester. It's here where I first encountered the life-altering power of the Spirit. As I began to take steps of faith and looked to count the cost of following Christ, a couple of friends and myself met one evening after college to seek God. We didn't hear the sound of a violent wind or witness what might appear like tongues of fire resting on our heads. But we knew the presence of God as our hearts burned within us much like those disciples on the Emmaus Road.

I had never felt such a love of Christ and such a passion to serve him. The desire to stay in that moment of encounter was strong, but the urgency to go was far stronger. I was compelled to leave. Not for home but for nations—to the least, the last, and the lost.

I knew I had received the Holy Spirit and with his presence came a missionary call; I am confident that these two things are inseparable. I was convinced I would head to India or Estonia or some other place that my limited geography could yet name. In discerning my assignment, two things began to emerge. Firstly, I was to cross the street before I was to cross any ocean. Secondly, I was being called to return to those I had run from. My calling was to become a domestic missionary, and my nation was those I had feared throughout my school years.

My family had moved to Manchester when I was twelve. We lived on the outer edge of an outer estate, and I always felt like an outsider. My school (named 'Druggie High' by the local press) was located between two disadvantaged communities, and I feared them both. I had planned my escape to middle-class suburbia, and my route out was upward mobility. I'd better myself with a good education. I'd pursue a good job. I'd move to a good place. Buy a guard dog. Build a wall.

My conservatory conversion turned my world upside down. God was calling me to downward mobility with a call to serve the disadvantaged in my own city—to give the best of myself to those experiencing the pain of poverty. I confess that this felt as costly as a one-way ticket to Mumbai.

As I began to explore urban mission, I heard about the Eden Network, a ministry of the Message Trust. They were pioneering something radical. They were sending out and supporting teams or urban missionaries in the most disadvantaged neighbourhoods—to live sacrificially, share the gospel, and build authentic community. I was confident of my calling, and I could see that Eden would provide me with the experience, encouragement, and equipping I would need to fulfil all that God had asked.

Nineteen years ago, I moved into a two-up, two-down terrace in Openshaw, East Manchester. Openshaw is a notorious estate but beautifully known by God. A community ranked high on the scale of deprivation but highly favoured by the Father. I am at home here. God has been faithful, and I continue to work with him in his mission among his people.[6]

A Spirit-filled People

Jon Tyson is a church leader in New York. We were recently at a gathering of global leaders with him, and he said that 'In scripture the more secular it got, the more supernatural it got. If your goal is the presence of God then you aren't linked in to a formula.' This so inspired us as our secular landscape is getting tough, and so maybe the best counterfoil for that is a greater move of the Spirit that will look, sound, and smell so distinct from the culture. As the secular narrative rises, so too must a Christian move of the supernatural.

In Zechariah 4 we have that famous verse, 'not by might nor by power, but by my Spirit' says the Lord' (v. 6). This verse is the absolute focal point of this vision. Why? Anything that could possibly be achieved by this group returning from exile would only have any impact at all by the power of the Spirit. If they were to rely on their own skills, gifts, strength, and resources then the whole thing would be a big waste of everyone's time. Relying solely on human resources and strength, their efforts would be worthless.[7] They had previously tried to rebuild the temple by their own strength straight after returning from Babylon over sixteen years earlier, but that turned out to be a an absolute farce (Ezra 3:8-13).

Why would it be any different for us today? Anything we hope to do must be fuelled by the power of the Spirit. As we seek to impact our land, we want to do so in step with what the Lord is already doing. Pete Hughes, who leads KXC church in London, puts it this way: 'We don't have a map, we have plans and strategies but we hold them lightly. Our one job is to stay as close as to the presence of God. This comes from prayer and a belief that the Spirit will lead us to be renewers of culture.'

An Urgent People

God is calling us to be a brave and Spirit-filled people, but he is also calling us to get going. The time is now for the church to rise up and make a difference in this land. We can wait for others to do so, but it is for us to act. We are forever hearing of how bad the world is, how everything is going down the drain, and how hope is eroding. There's a simple solution: change it. The world is not transformed by political slogans and trending Twitter hashtags but by people making a difference, rolling their sleeves up, and living differently from the landscape around them. A bunch of Christians prepared to be influencers, not the influenced, and happy to make a huge impact.

In many ways it can feel like the church in the UK is asleep whilst the darkness appears to be winning and taking advantage of our slumber. R. T. Kendal is convinced that the UK church is asleep. He says that 'The greatest evidence that we are asleep is our lack of outrage over what is tolerated in the church and what is going on in the world. Not only are we indifferent to what is happening before our eyes, we have become so used to it that we are virtually impervious to it. The biblical view of marriage is on the way out. Terrorism is at our doors. Church attendance is declining more than ever. We are losing our young people. If someone calls things like this to our attention we say, "Oh yes. It's pretty awful." Then we roll over. Zzzzzzzz. "Let me sleep on."[8]

We need to wake up, rise up, and become urgent for the sake of the Gospel. We never know when the Lord will return, but we must live each day in expectation that it's soon. Like the Acts church before us, we need to lay it all on the line and get moving, sharing with all around us.

Maybe we need to get dangerous and brave again, knowing that he will be with us, empowering us through the Spirit. Perhaps you're a little distracted and have lost sight of the main thing. Maybe it's all gotten a bit safe for you. We need to ensure that our walk with Jesus is the light by which we see everything else. That his will is the driving force behind our lives. That we go where he wants, are brave if he says so, and see the things around us in the light of his glory and not forget that he is central to everything.

We find the chorus from a famous old hymn really inspiring.

Turn your eyes upon Jesus,
Look full in His wonderful face,
And the things of earth will grow strangely dim,
In the light of His glory and grace.

Yes, but How?

For you:
- Would you describe yourself as brave?
- What scares you the most?
- What does God say about that?

For your group:
Have a look at Esther 4 and talk together about how Esther responds to what is in front of her.

1 How would you feel in her shoes?
2 What would you do?
3 Do you think you could be as brave as she was, given the opportunity?

A change of emphasis?
Our fellow Spring Harvest leader, Cris Rogers, really challenged us both recently. He said that when it comes to being unleashed many of us need to change our intentionality, not just do more. When it comes to our efforts, he says that we need to look for things that are low maintenance, high impact, not high maintenance, low impact.

Where might we need to change our emphasis for a greater output?

Further Reading:
G. Fee, *God's Empowering Presence* (Peabody: Hendrickson, 2009)
S. Ponsonby, *More* (Colorado Springs: David C. Cook, 2010)
M. Duncan, *Risk-Takers* (Oxford: Monarch Books, 2013)
J. I. Packer, *Keep in Step with the Spirit* (Grand Rapids: Baker Books, 2005)

Part 2

UNLEASHED PEOPLE

Acts 2:42–47 and 4:32–37

Acts 2:42-47

The Fellowship of the Believers

They devoted themselves to the apostles' teaching and to fellowship, to the breaking of bread and to prayer. [43]Everyone was filled with awe at the many wonders and signs performed by the apostles. 44 All the believers were together and had everything in common. [45]They sold property and possessions to give to anyone who had need. [46]Every day they continued to meet together in the temple courts. They broke bread in their homes and ate together with glad and sincere hearts, [47]praising God and enjoying the favour of all the people. And the Lord added to their number daily those who were being saved.

Acts 4:32-37

The Believers Share Their Possessions

All the believers were one in heart and mind. No one claimed that any of their possessions was their own, but they shared everything they had. [33]With great power the apostles continued to testify to the resurrection of the Lord Jesus. And God's grace was so powerfully at work in them all [34] that there were no needy persons among them. For from time to time those who owned land or houses sold them, brought the money from the sales [35] and put it at the apostles' feet, and it was distributed to anyone who had need.

[36]Joseph, a Levite from Cyprus, whom the apostles called Barnabas (which means "son of encouragement"), [37]sold a field he owned and brought the money and put it at the apostles' feet.

4

Independent Living

'If we have no peace, it is because we have forgotten that we belong to each other.'

Mother Theresa

A Different Way?

It was a lovely summer's morning as the train pulled slowly into the small station of Robertsbridge, East Sussex. We love living in London, but it's wonderful sometimes to get away from the hustle and bustle of it all and instead spend some time in the green fields of England. I, Gavin, was off to experience a day amongst the Bruderhof community there. The Bruderhof are an evangelical Christian movement that base so much of what they practice on the early church as described in the first few chapters of the book of Acts. They have communities all over the world, and believe in sharing everything fully; they are peacemakers and passionate proclaimers of the gospel. The community as a whole raises their children, everyone cares for the elderly, the discipleship of all is a community activity, and all possessions are shared. It really is quite something.

The community was amazing. I was picked up by one of the leaders who had use of one of the shared cars to pick me up. As we pulled into the car park within the community, there was an overwhelming sense of peace. The place was like an oasis of calm and the sense of God was palpable. Straight away my host returned the car keys to a central point. He could see my confusion so quickly said, 'We have to return the keys as there are just a few cars between us all, and I don't

47

want the next person to not have them on time.' I instantly felt guilty for the times I moan about Anne and me sharing a car.

I met many of the community and was blown away by their warmth, contentment, and joy. Moreover, their devotion to Jesus was remarkable, and yet they felt it to be normal. Here were people living like the early church but in today's Britain. This was not another nation or continent; I had been on a short train journey from London and yet it felt like I was half the world away from home. No one independently owned anything; each member of the community was supported by all people within it, and self-sacrifice from all was evident. It was a pleasure to be amongst them.

As the day continued, I felt a number of questions rising up in me—from the profound to the fairly ludicrous. My guide was only too happy to answer anything. 'What happens when people fall out?' 'Well, they have to resolve their differences in a godly way.' 'What do young people do about dating?' 'We work through those kind of things as a community.' 'What do you do about getting new shoes?' 'If you need them then you let your shoe size be known by the community leaders, and they get you a pair in that size.' 'What happens when you retire?' 'You don't. Everyone contributes to community life as much as they can, irrespective of age.' 'What if a couple gets divorced?' 'That has not happened yet.' 'What do your kids want for Christmas?' 'That is the strangest question yet. Why would they want anything for Christmas? We aren't consumers in that way. They get some sweets and a wooden toy or similar made in the workshop.'

This was a totally different way of living. At first it was hugely appealing, but as my day drew to a close I realised how hard it would be to live like this. I asked what it would mean for my family to join and was told that we would have to be certain as it would involve us selling our home, and just about all we own, and giving the proceeds to the community. We would then live as part of the Bruderhof for the rest of our lives and could be moved around to different communities all over the planet if the leaders felt this beneficial or the Lord's will.

Our children would, in turn, be part of the community and when they became adults would have a choice to make about being part of it for life too. I'm embarrassed to admit that I stood there thinking how much I'd miss my own front door to hide behind, the freedom to make my own spiritual and financial decisions, the chance to choose which things to own, and my overall sense of independence.

The whole episode set my mind racing. As the train headed back to London, I had all sorts of questions running through my head. I have been so westernized with a self-centred worldview that my encounter with this incredible godly community had shown me that there was another way. Why do we live on a street where there are at least four Christian families who don't share anything? How have we moved so far away from the model of the early church where everyone took care of one another? Does my individual pension plan really matter more than caring for others? Regrettably, joining the Bruderhof is probably a step too far for us, but we can't go on allowing the world to permit us to be so self-absorbed when we are called to be a family.

The Church Today

One of the biggest problems that the church faces in the UK is us. Yes, that's right, 'you and me'. The western media has worked very hard to equip us to think about ourselves and what we want, what we can achieve, and who we are. Nothing is more important than 'me'. We have been encouraged to live for ourselves and to only count on Number One.

A couple of years ago I, Anne, was preparing my notes for a conference and asking the Lord to graciously share his heart for his people. It's one thing to share eloquent or humorous words, but bringing a sense of God's heart does not just entertain but breathes life and transformation to a group of his children. There are times when we feel that there is a clear sense of what the Spirit might be saying, other moments when we have to wait, and somewhere we just go in faith and trust that what we bring will be applicable to the listeners' lives.

In this time of preparation there was a constant impression in my mind of a very large person sitting in an armchair. It was quite a repulsive image to see because the individual was consuming large amounts of food and drink without stopping. They were totally engrossed in what they were feeding on next and completely unaware of how large they were growing. Bits of food were building up around the person's mouth and drink was dribbling down their chin, but still they kept eating and gulping. I kept asking God to take away the picture because it was so horrible I didn't think it was from him. However, if anything, it just became more prominent and grotesque in my mind. The more I saw the image the more detail I could see, and the one thing that became very clear was that the person had reached a point where they could not move out of the chair. When they held on to the arms of the chair to try and lift their now extreme body weight out of the seat, the fat prevented them from standing up; they were totally stuck into the seat. The saddest thing I observed was that the person did not, at this point, stop consuming. They just carried on as if nothing bad was happening to them.

After about a week of seeing this across my mind's eye every single day, I felt increasingly sick and asked the Lord, 'What is this? Please, if it's not from you, take it away!' So far the prayer had just been 'Take it away, Lord,' but as I asked 'What is it?' I believe I heard a response from him: 'This is what some of my church looks like, Anne.' It was a short, clear, simple sentence, but it caused me to fall to my face in tears and cry out: 'What, are you kidding me? But this is repulsive, Father. Surely we don't look like this?' I began to weep tears of repentance and repeatedly utter the refrain, 'I'm so sorry, I'm so sorry, I'm so sorry.' I knelt on the hard kitchen floor asking, 'Lord are we really consumers? Are we really oblivious to getting stuck? Are we that unaware of the world around us, of how what we are doing is slowly killing us?' No answer. 'Yes, yes, yes' just rang through my guts. After a long time I became aware of very sore knees and eyes; I simply said, 'Help us, Jesus.'

Sitting in a more comfortable position, but still on the floor, I dried my eyes, opened the Bible, and began to pray some more: 'Lord what do we do? What can we do to get moving again, to stop consuming like this? We cannot do it ourselves.' These short questions and cries to God have often been the most life-changing moments in my journey with him. He doesn't just love our thoughts but the opportunity to dialogue with us, to respond as well as listen.

Drawn to John chapter 21, I began to read part of the post resurrection narrative again—the awesome reality of the risen Lord Jesus appearing to his disciples before he ascends into heaven. This time he arrives on the beach whilst Peter and the others are out fishing. He gives them another miraculous catch of fish and then invites them to share breakfast with him. Peter jumps into the water, the man who denied his Lord three times and watched him die, is now desperate to be with him again. Aren't we funny people? We say we love him and want to follow, but how far are we really willing to go? Jesus must have been broken hearted when he realized that one of his closest followers would turn his back on him, and then here he is running through the water back to him.

After breakfast, Jesus confronts Peter. However, he addresses him as Simon, as the rock had failed to live up to his name.[1] 'Simon, son of John, do you love me more than these?' 'Yes Lord, you know that I love you.' Jesus said, 'Feed my lambs.' Again Jesus said, 'Simon, son of John, do you love me?' He answered, 'Yes Lord you know that I love you. Jesus said, 'Take care of my sheep.' The third time Jesus said to him, 'Simon, son of John, do you love me?' Peter was hurt because Jesus asked him a third time, 'Do you love me?' He said, 'Lord you know all things, you know that I love you.' Jesus said 'Feed my sheep' (John 21:15-17).

Again and again Jesus focused on the same thing: 'Peter, do you love me?' He wants to reinstate his son and the way he does it is by asking this question. I dwelt on these words for a while, trying to make sense of them alongside the detestable image of the person in the chair. 'Lord', I muttered again, 'what has this got to do with that picture?'

Another simple sentence came flooding into my mind:

'Stop feeding yourselves and start feeding others.'

Wow. Those words have stuck so strongly in our hearts and minds:

'*Stop* feeding yourselves and *start* feeding others.'

How much do we love Jesus? How much do we really want to follow him? When Peter denies Jesus, it's because he became afraid. He started to think about himself and what will happen to him, rather than focusing on his God. This is the problem we have too: we think about ourselves ahead of him, ahead of others. The media says 'Pursue comfort, be consumers, and you will be happy,' but in actual fact, the message of Jesus is 'Take up your cross and follow me' (Matthew 16:24). That's the way to life and 'Come as far as you can towards Calvary—keep dying to self.' The more we love him ahead of anything else, the further we can go with him because we will put him ahead of everything else. Jesus isn't saying to the western church that they shouldn't take care of their families, but he is saying 'Seek *me first* and my kingdom and everything else will be added to you' (Matthew 6:33, paraphrased).

By the end of that morning of prayer and revelation, the remaining cry of my heart was 'Lord, show me what I am consumed by. Show us what is keeping us stuck where we are. Help us to love you more, to know you more, to have a greater hunger in our hearts for you, over and above our hunger for the things of the world. Lord, help me to want to feed your sheep more than I desire to feed myself.'

The western church are in a 'wake up and get moving' season, and the Lord is lifting our eyes off of ourselves and onto his face and his mission. He is revealing different things to many different people to show us what we need to stop doing and start doing to press in for his kingdom to come and will be done.

It starts with us on our faces.

The problem is that because we have put ourselves on the throne of our lives, there is no room for God and there is no real room for others. The challenge is that because we are often looking to please ourselves, church becomes a consumer temple that will never satisfy our needs. Some church leaders are desperately trying to please the 'me mentality' within our churches: bright lights, nicer coffee, comfy chairs, a good programme. They are managing to appease the consumer for a time, as long as they keep updating the place and bring fresh ideas that will satisfy our desires. Francis Chan highlights this challenge: 'It's no secret that most people who attend church services come as consumers rather than servants.'[2]

The Early Church

So when we turn our thoughts to Acts again and read chapter 4:32-37, it is with our consumer mentality in mind. We literally see the completely opposite mindset being worked out. It is not about us, it is about them; it is not what we want, but what they need. 'All the believers were one in heart and mind. No one claimed that any of his possessions was his own, but they shared everything they had' (4:32-33). And this is not the first time that Luke refers to their togetherness. He has already commented on it in Acts 2, the move of the Spirit has brought a powerful sense of togetherness that is infectious to the outside world. 'All the believers were together and had everything in common. Selling their possessions and goods, they gave to anyone as he had need' (Acts 2:44-45). Ajith Fernando helpfully comments: 'Saying it twice tells us how important it is. This shared life wasn't an end in itself, because what united these people was their commitment to a mission: spreading the news of Jesus. And unlike modern communism, the sharing of wealth was voluntary (though generous) and private ownership continued.'[3]

We do not witness an individualistic thought process but a unity, a togetherness across the community that the Lord uses to advance the gospel. This is a very practical application of the Greek word *koinonia*, meaning that these Christians held everything in common for the sake of the wider world.[4] In some incredibly powerful way the Holy Spirit draws them together so that they move together as one, like the Godhead. The early followers are a true living answer to the prayer that Jesus prays in John 17:21, 'that all of them may be one, Father, just as you are in me and I am in you.' This unity is so that 'the world will know that you sent me and have loved them even as you have loved me' (17:23). The togetherness that we see is so powerful that it draws the lost to Jesus: the King is at work—Father, Son, and Holy Spirit—in order to draw people to Christ. And it works! 'The Lord added to their number daily those who were being saved' (Acts 2:47).

The Fellowship of the Believers

Following Pentecost and Peter's incredibly powerful words, we find ourselves being given, as John Stott says, 'A beautiful little cameo of the Spirit-filled Church.'[5] It's interesting to note what was actually involved in early church life. There appear to be four things noted in Acts 2:42-47. Another commentator notes that 'a case can be made out that they are in fact the four elements which character-ized a Christian gathering in the early church.'[6] Church comprised of teaching, fellowship, breaking bread, and prayer. This makes us pause in our tracks for a moment: Is this what church is character-ized by now? Maybe we are doing these things but how central are they? These things were at the heart of everything, and at the heart of them was a radical love for Jesus and for one another.

When you read that the apostles 'devoted' themselves to the apostles' teaching and to the fellowship, to the breaking of bread and to prayer (2:42), we are left asking, 'What would cause them to do that?', The dictionary definition of 'devoted' is 'very loving and loyal.' Through encounter with Jesus, the power of the Holy Spirit had expressed itself with this incredible love and commitment to one another—a radical, embracing, endless, faithful, consistent love that could have only be imparted from the Lord himself. The fact that they were totally devoted to the apostles' teaching reveals an insatiable hunger that had suddenly incurred as a result of the Risen Jesus being proclaimed and the power of the Spirit received. We long to see that kind of love, that sort of community, that depth of hunger spilled out across the church, with the truth being that no one and nothing can satisfy like Jesus.

As we read a bit further down, it is mind-blowing to read that they 'sold property and possessions to give to anyone who had need' (2:45). It is also mirrored in Acts 4:32: 'No one claimed that any of their possessions was their own, but they shared everything they had.' Does this mean we need to start emptying our homes of what we own and give it all away? No, it does not. This way of living is voluntary. We are also made aware that some of the believers still had houses: 'They broke bread in their homes and ate together with glad and sincere hearts' (2:46). 'What is described is a voluntary sharing of possessions based on the deep sense of fellowship.'[7] There was still a sense of some independent living, but what is perhaps more vital to highlight is 'how' they looked on what they owned: there was a definite sense that they held every possession lightly and prayerfully before the throne of God, willing to sacrifice to see others receive. We witness a radical generosity amongst the early believers that was infectious because it radiated profound love in an oppressive, contested environment. What might that look like in our landscape in the UK?

We must also note that in the midst of this powerful togetherness there was also a sense of fear as 'everyone was filled with awe at the many wonders and signs performed by the apostles.' (2:43). There was a sense of wonder as the people witnessed wonders, a deep awareness of God at work, perhaps a constant acknowledgment that God was present and it was only because of him that lives were being saved and transformed. 'That awe was only increased as the power of the Spirit was at work through the apostles' as it had been with Jesus, power to heal and transform people's lives.'[8]

The more we read, the more we long to make sure we have the four components of fellowship, teaching, prayer, and breaking bread at the core of church life. However, what feels far more important and necessary than just going through the motions of doing these things is asking the love of Jesus, by the power of his Spirit, to breathe through every bit of what we are doing. Will we not then naturally be a 'learning church, a loving church, a worshipping church and an evangelistic church'[9] that is equipped and ready to welcome many into the kingdom?

The Spring Harvest team were reflecting on one of the recent conferences at Butlins and sharing stories of all that the Lord had been doing. Apparently, one of the managers of the Butlins holiday resorts had asked to look around one of the sites, to see the different venues to get a flavour for what was happening. He was suddenly intrigued by this large Christian gathering filling the resort. Towards the end of his tour around the site, he turned to one of our team and said that what really stood out was the fact that everyone was clearly there for the same reason—there was a togetherness, a unity of purpose that he could not ignore. When we gather to scatter, there is power beyond what we might see. The staff at Butlins likes to work during the weeks of Spring Harvest—who knows what difference this has made over the years! As we continued to review during that planning meeting, our prayer was that these testimonies would continue and that our togetherness would draw many to Christ.

Turning back to our own churches, how much do they look like what we read here in Acts 2 and 4? Can you imagine church not being an hour and a half service on a Sunday that many of us struggle to commit to and rather a gathering of believers meeting regularly, perhaps more spontaneously, with such a hunger in their hearts not only to be together but to serve one another: a group of people eager to give up their own land and houses (4:34) for the sake of others?

Wouldn't it be incredible if together there could be a greater Spirit-inspired move away from pleasing ourselves to pleasing God and other people?

Jesus said that he 'didn't come to be served but to serve.' His whole life was an act of service. The more like Christ we become, the more servant-hearted we are. However, what we do not see here in Acts is a church operating out of duty, but out of joy. They are powerfully moved by the love of God in their hearts to share with their brothers and sisters. There is an overflow of generosity, of kindness, and self-lessness that spills forth in the early church.

'They devoted themselves to the apostles' teaching and to fellowship, to the breaking of bread and to prayer. Everyone was filled with awe at the many wonders and signs performed by the apostles. All the believers were together and had everything in common' (Acts 2:42-44).

The believers were meeting together daily in the temple courts; they were sold out for Jesus and for one another. Isn't this an incredible picture? Can you imagine feeling like you have everything in common with the other people in your church? This community of believers were so in love with God, so filled with the Spirit that it felt like they were family, and they were all living for the same purpose.

The Iranian Church

When I, Anne, was in Turkey having the privilege of ministering amongst the Iranian church, it was one of the most life-changing moments of my walk with Jesus. There were four of us in total there to gather three churches together and teach, pray, and share fellowship. I so distinctly remember our first time of gathered sung worship. We began to sing 'Here I am, down on my knees again, surrendering all' in Farsi, and the power of the Holy Spirit was so strong I was compelled to go down on my face. As I did it, I thought 'Here I am again, making a scene in a worship time' (I always want to physically respond), but I was obedient to the urge in my guts. After a short while, I raised my head and looked around. Normally I would find I was the only one and would shuffle quickly and quietly back up to my feet, but in this instance I was overwhelmed. Every single person was down on their knees worshipping with all of their hearts. So many adult men with tears in their eyes, singing with all that they had in them. I found my eyes welling up, and it felt like I had come home.

The Iranian church, together, every single one of them, together in worship, one heart and one mind, desperately hungry for Jesus and seeking him with all that they had. It was like what we imagine the early church to be. The only place they wanted to be was at the feet of Jesus, and in those few days in Turkey, the Lord was adding to their number daily those who were being saved.

After a long day of meeting together, praying, and worshipping, we finally went out for food at approximately 11 p.m. These guys could have happily gone without food; it was the nagging Brits that made them think with their stomachs. Anyway, in the Kebab restaurant the team just began to share the gospel, and everywhere we went they were handing out New Testaments and talking about Jesus. The infectious passion, the church filled with the Holy Spirit, kept compelling them to share the love of God; it was so deeply challenging.

Coming home from this experience there was a deep realization that we can encounter the love of God together in a way that we had only really known on our own with the Lord. Our jobs, cars, commutes, busyness, devices, hobbies, etc., are great, but how often do they remove us from real relationship? They can obviously be amazing ways to engage with people, but how often is our schedule stealing real relationship with those that God is calling us to?

It seems that the enemy is intent on using any means possible to stop the extension of the kingdom of God, and so he will distract us with as many things as he can so that we cannot connect to God or to one another. If the greatest commandment is to 'Love the Lord your

God with all your heart, soul, mind, and strength and to love your neighbour as yourself,' then the enemy will do whatever he can to try and stop you loving the Lord and loving your neighbour. Stealing our stillness seems to be a number one tactic in the west right now.

There is something beautiful that God wants to do that is not just about the Iranian church (although they are modelling something powerful), it is about the whole church of Jesus Christ across the whole world. He is calling us to a unity that might feel uncomfortable and messy and risky, but it is so that he can display his glory and draw others to himself. The massive challenge that comes to us in the west is this: 'It demands everything—hopes, plans, time, money, and energy—and can even cost our lives. It should come as no surprise then, really, that unbelievers analyse the lives of Christians around them to decide if their gospel is true. This is one of the reasons that the early church grew so rapidly, and it may be the reason why the western church is declining just as rapidly too.'[10]

If we begin to model a togetherness that loves one another more than we love ourselves, that serves each other at a cost, we will begin to see the lost attracted to the gospel and to Jesus, because at the heart of our faith is sacrifice, born out of love. This, we believe, is not just about gathering in our churches to love one another, not just feasting and worshipping and praying behind closed doors, but a 'togetherness' that is demonstrated in the workplace or at school.

One friend of ours gathers Christians from different churches to pray in the primary school, another friend of ours does meal rotas for two weeks, not just for the women in the church who give birth, but also for women who attend the mums and tots or are part of the preschool. A story that really challenged us was a prayer meeting movement that began in New York many years ago: 'Jeremiah began a lunch time prayer meeting for businessmen. On the first day after praying alone for thirty minutes, he was joined by five people. The following week twenty arrived, and on the third week there were forty and then one hundred...by January 1858, there were

50,000 people in New York who were praying at noon in one hundred prayer meetings across the city...prayer meetings were also begun in Philadelphia, Chicago, and beyond.'[11] This was happening in the workplace! People together as living demonstrations of the power of the gospel and the Lord was moving in power.

The question is: how is God calling us to unite? To gather his people in an infectious way that is a living demonstration of him at work?

Yes, but How?

For you:

- What are you hungry for? We all have an appetite for something. Are you hungry for God? For his mission? We will not be satisfied fully by anything other than God.
- Jesus says to Peter, 'Feed my sheep.' Who is he calling you to feed?

For your group:

- The Bruderhof demonstrate an incredible way of community living. As you hear that story and read the Acts narrative of togetherness, are you challenged about how you live? If so, in what areas specifically?
- Why not brainstorm some ways in which we could operate as the body of Christ more effectively? Perhaps there are tangible ways you are already seeing in your area?
- This might be a good moment to pause and pray: 'Lord show us how to feed your sheep, and how to love one another in a way that seeks to serve rather than be served.'

Further Reading:

S. Ponsonby, *Different: Living the Holy Life* (London: Hodder & Stoughton, 2016)

A. Fernando, *Jesus Driven Ministry* (Leicester: IVP, 2002)

5

Living As One

'One of the main tasks we have is to find words that do not divide but unite, that do not create conflict but unity, that do not hurt but heal.'

Henri Nouwen

Family

We are part of a wonderful global family, with many who have gone before, and many who are yet to come. We are part of a body that began over two thousand years ago, was empowered by the Holy Spirit, and goes on being equipped and released today. The story is not finished yet and won't be until Jesus comes again. We are a body, and if one part of the body is not working, then we are all the poorer for it. The body is not made up of one part, but of many. It's in our differences that we are more useful too. It's brilliant; we are not all the same, as diversity is needed in function, character, and output. We may not be the same, but we are called to be united. Paul puts it this way in 1 Corinthians 12, verses 17-19: 'If the whole body were an eye, where would the sense of hearing be? If the whole body were an ear, where would the sense of smell be? But in fact God has placed the parts in the body, every one of them, just as he wanted them to be. If they were all one part, where would the body be?' We need each other, and it's the different roles we play whilst remaining one body that makes the church so formidable.

There are many reasons why we might not work with others, such as suspicion, mistrust, or lack of relationship. But our differences must not stop our unity. The former general director of the Evangelical Alliance (EA), Steve Clifford, puts it this way, 'Church will come in all kinds of shapes and sizes and cultural expressions, but it is still the Church – The followers of Jesus coming together to fulfil His purposes in the world.'[1] One key area for this would be in ethnic diversity. The Evangelical Alliance's One People Commission has seen significant bridges built across previous ethnic boundaries.[2] As the senior pastor of Jesus House in London and the UK overseer of the Redeemed Christian Church of God (RCCG), Pastor Agu Irukwu said recently to a bunch of white leaders, 'We're brothers with the same Father but different mothers!' As it says in Galatians 3:28, 'There is neither Jew nor Gentile, neither slave nor free, nor is there male and female, for you are all one in Christ Jesus.' We are one body.

In recent years I, Gavin, have been privileged to find myself speaking in many different cultural contexts within the UK church. A great help in this has been my dear friend and brother, Yemi Adedeji. We have shared platforms in different settings, and Yemi has been a real gift in helping me understand certain cultural differences and actions in the UK church. It has been a real pleasure and a delight to see the Lord on the move powerfully across so many ethnicities. From small south Asian churches to being translated into Korean, to speaking at a prayer meeting of over 10,000 people at the Excel arena where there were about ten other white folks, the ethnic diversity of the church in the UK is an absolute wonder to behold. Equally, I, Gavin, get to minister in churches where most people are of the same ethnicity but where something like the music is totally different, or the practice not what I'm used to, and yet there is something glorious about the differences. We are naturally charismatic, and yet there is something to be appreciated in worshipping in a church that isn't every so often. We must avoid confusing style with substance. The substance belongs to the Lord and we must not change that, but the style can change like the wind.

The incredible thing is that we remain one body in Christ even though we sometimes do things differently. In heaven there will not be separate sections for different ages, races, genders, or anything else. We will all be united in worshipping for eternity. We need to do all we can to embrace being part of a dynamic and diverse body of Christ in the UK now. We held a men's curry night from our church in the curry house on our street. There were twenty-two men there from fifteen different ethnicities and ranging in age from teenager to retired. The guy who runs the curry house asked me, Gavin, what the group was. I asked in return what he thought it was. The gentleman answered, 'The church.' I asked why and he said 'For a start you're a vicar type, Gav, but more importantly, who else could get such a diverse group of people to all have a meal together? You had to be the church.' That is so encouraging. In an increasingly fractured culture, we can bring all kinds of people together as the one family that we are. Who else can bring such a diverse people together other than the church? It's utterly wonderful.

One

We find it impossible to talk about the work of God without acknowledging the vital need for us to 'be one.' Even the God that we follow is part of a 'God-head' with the Father, Son, and Holy Spirit deeply and intimately connected, yet reflecting different aspects of our Lord. Unity is not just a good idea, it's a Christian essential and Jesus prays it for his church in John 17. This chapter underpins so much of Gavin's work at the EA and has been foundational there for years. It's a prayer that is inspiring but deeply challenging, especially if we put the words of it into practice. The theologian Tom Wright puts it this way: 'When you make this prayer your own, when you enter into this chapter and see what happens, you are being invited to come into the heart of that intimate relation between Jesus and the Father and have it, so to speak, happen all around you. This is both what the prayer embodies and also its central subject matter.'[3]

Jesus is just about to be arrested and yet his focus is on praying for all believers that they will be 'one'. He obviously considered it very important. With all that he was facing, with the mission in front of him and the immediacy of his task, Jesus prayed this prayer in John 17. The church pastor Malcolm Duncan puts it this way" 'In one of the most difficult moments of His entire ministry, with the cross looming before Him and guards on the way to arrest Him, He asked His Father that we would be one.'[4] This unity is that important.

Jesus prays for the disciples and for all those who will believe through his message (17:6-26). When Jesus prays for protection for the disciples, he is praying that they might be 'one as we are one' (17:11)—as one like the Godhead, in order to reflect the Lord to non-believers. He goes on: 'I have given them the glory that you gave me, that they may be one as we are one—I in them and you in me—so that they may be brought to complete unity. Then the world will know that you sent me and have loved them even as you have loved me.' (17:22-23).

When you reflect on centuries past, we see a church continually unsure over whether it could be 'one' as Jesus prayed we would. David King, who looked at local unity in Scotland in the middle of the nineteenth century, pressed and stressed the need for 'unity, as Christ prayed for it, to be visible so that the world might believe. Unity was simply a means, with the end being people coming to faith in Christ.'[5] This kind of desire for unity has been the lifeblood of the Evangelical Alliance ever since it's formation in 1846.

Thankfully, this unity is not dependent on us; God is at work in us by his Holy Spirit. The theologian R. V. G. Tasker puts it helpfully: 'This unity, like the love which produces it, is supernatural; it is fundamentally the same as the unity that exists between Father and Son...The perfection of this unity will only be reached so long as the believers keep in touch with their exalted Lord and contemplate the glory which has been His from eternity.'[6] It's hard to maintain this unity but we must do all we can to fight for it. It's this unity that the world will notice and be drawn to. In his commentary on John's gospel, Bruce Milne says when reflecting on John 17 that the church must be united, that this unity must be tangible so that the world sees, grasps, and is impacted by it, and that this unity must be directed outwards so that the world may come to know Jesus too.[7] This unity is not a great secret for us to keep to ourselves but a powerful part of fulfilling the Great Commission.

On the ground throughout the land, there are hugely encouraging signs of growing Christian unity that is making a huge impact. This has been seen greatly in England through the work of Gather that seeks to celebrate and catalyse unity in communities. It's leader, Roger Sutton, writes 'When the Church of God begins to see itself as one body across a city or town, when it begins to pray and relate in close friendship across denominational lines, when its ordinary members begin to see themselves as God's agents of change and form relational and strategic networks across the spheres of society, when Christians begin to own and love the places they are sent to and develop an all-encompassing transformational vision, then something very significant is happening.'[8]

All Ages

Our unity must span across all generations too. Have you ever watched the programme where the parents go away for a week and the kids are left to turn the family home into whatever they wish? It's an absolutely crazy philosophy, and anyway, who in their right mind does that? Some people obviously. You sit and watch the poor returning parents looking totally horrified as they observe their once beautifully decorated lounge transformed into a window-less cinema, their spacious kitchen replaced with a burger bar, and their antique four-poster bed swapped for individual sleeping pods. The look of utter desperation on their faces somehow makes you want to laugh and cry in equal measure. Laugh because they were nuts enough to agree to it, and cry because you know how you would feel if it happened to you.

The whole notion of the programme made us wonder what might

happen if the adult church decided to willingly go away for a week, allowing the teenagers to reform the church into what they wanted it to be. Can you picture what might happen? Would it be as disastrous as the programme? We have to say that we would find it incredibly exciting, but we know there are many churchgoers who would be terrified by such a suggestion. The more we thought about it, the more aware we became of how different the generations are. How the hopes and desires of young people for the church are often very different to the older attendees, and as a sad result, they can frequently feel like outsiders in the one place they should call home.

If a young family were to download a film to watch together, the choice will always reflect the preferences of the least mature. Dad may desperately want to watch *Rambo*, but his five-year-old daughter and seven-year-old son would definitely find *Dumbo* to be more appealing and appropriate. Inevitably, common sense dictates that Dad settles down to watch the Disney film with his children. Why then do all the rules change when it comes to church life? Why on earth do we expect less mature teenagers to integrate into our adult way of doing church? Surely this situation should be entirely reversed. The more mature adult Christians should make every effort to integrate with those younger in the faith. This will not always be an age thing. If a number of people become Christians at a later stage of life, then they too need accommodating in a similar way.

The more spiritually mature should sacrifice their own preferences and not expect the less mature to do so. It's time we started seeing church as a true family and reflecting this in all we do. In our own lives, when our parents came to visit us before we had kids, we would get a takeaway curry and watch an episode of *Poirot*. You can't get much more middle-aged than that! However, when grandchildren came along, suddenly the grandparents were happy to have McDonalds and watch *Peppa Pig*. Why? Because it bought joy to the youngest members of the family and included everyone. It was not the grandparents' style or choice, but the family had a new generation now and so the overall unit adjusted accordingly. Surely, the same should be true within the church family. Maybe achieving this fully and quickly is a little unrealistic, but we honestly believe that if some of the more established Christians compromised a little to meet the less mature in the middle, then the future of the church would look a great deal brighter.

Whether we like it or not, young people are going to struggle within the confines of the church. As teenagers they are going to want to break out and discover new things for themselves. The problem is not in the struggle, but in how the church chooses to respond. We need to create an environment that is youth friendly so that even when young people kick against a wall, we still welcome them in with open arms. This can be achieved in all kinds of ways from inviting them to have a say in church meetings, to playing sports together, to just having a conversation over a coffee. We need to do all we can to help younger people in their journey into faith.

There are so many incredible younger people out there desperately needing to hear about Jesus. The vast majority of those who come to faith are under age twenty-five (around 86%),[9] and we therefore need to put a great deal of our effort, resources, and prayers into younger generations. We can have such an impact too. There is a famous secular youth work quote that says 'it takes one significant adult to impact a young person's morality, worldview and lifestyle forever.' We can be these significant adults to a new generation. Encouragingly, many of the great Christian historical figures came to faith as young people. Charles Spurgeon (aged fifteen when he surrendered his life to Jesus), George Whitefield (sixteen), William Booth (fifteen), C. T. Studd (sixteen), James Hudson Taylor (fifteen), D. L. Moody (eighteen), Amy Carmichael (fifteen), and Billy Graham (seventeen).[10] Who knows what the young people in our communities could go on to do with our support?

We do need also to support those already within our churches. The old African proverb 'it takes a whole village to raise a child' can be similarly adapted to a church setting to say that it 'takes a whole village to raise a young person in the faith.' As parents, we are certainly hugely grateful to the many within our church who are helping to disciple our two kids. They are having a huge impact. The *Talking Jesus* research from the Barna group[11] showed that, by far, the number one way that people come to faith (41%) is by being born into a Christian home. Therefore, we must do all we can to support families in raising Christian children, especially in our fast and pressurized world.

A little while back, I, Gavin, met four wonderful women, all in their nineties, who were desperate to see the young people of their town reached for Jesus. They felt they had nothing to offer but wanted so much for the church to have a future. I talked with them about the great needs of young people and encouraged them to try to reach out. With the help of the team at Youth for Christ, who walked through the process with them, they bravely set up a youth group (a Rock Solid Club)[12] for those aged 11 to 14, arranging to meet once a week. Six months later I was thrilled to receive a letter from one of the women saying that there were now thirty young people coming to their youth group on a Thursday evening. As these old women prove, it doesn't matter what your age; anyone can bridge that gap. It just takes a heart of compassion for young people and a desire to see the church have a future. We are never too old to be unleashed, be it inside or outside the church building.

Let's be part of a church where all generations are working, loving, and serving so well together that the numbers of lost souls being saved is doubling every week, and we shut the back door so we don't lose those that we already have too. That's the church that we dream of.

Gifts

One of the beautiful hallmarks of this 'oneness' that we witness in Acts is the way that different gifts are being released and implemented side by side. Everyone seems to be playing their part within the body to see the Great Commission worked out. There is recognition of what people individually bring, who should be serving where, and then they get on and make it happen. And it is not just a question of 'Well, are they any good at that?' It involves knowing one another, loving each other, being prayerful, and listening to the leading of the Holy Spirit. In Acts 6 we witness the widows being overlooked in the daily distribution of food. They don't just choose practical people to sort it out, but those 'who are known to be full of the Spirit and wisdom' (6:3). There is a group who choose the Seven and present them to the apostles (6:5); there are the apostles focusing on prayer and ministry of the word (6:4); the actual Seven who resolve the problem (6:5): all God's children working together in different areas, affirmed and enabled. They don't just let them get on with it either: they lay hands on them and pray—this is as important as any other role, and there is always prayer (6:6). We see the same when Paul and Barnabas are set apart and sent off—more prayer (13:3).

God longs for this: to see every single one of his children involved and added to his mission, and every single part of the body affirmed and released and empowered to play its part. Over the years, we have given more focus to some people, we have allowed certain roles to carry greater weight than others, and we have put more work on the shoulders of those who seem willing to carry it. Francis Chan comments on his own previous church 'Cornerstone': 'When I looked at what went on in Cornerstone, I saw a few other people and me using our gifts, while thousands just came and sat in the sanctuary for an hour and a half and then went home. The way we had structured the church was stunting people's growth, and the whole body was weaker for it.'[13]

Equal

We believe that something is happening right now in our churches where the Lord is reminding us that hierarchy was never part of his plan, that none of us are more 'called' than any other, even if we are ordained! The Spirit is at work in the grassroots to wake everyone up, to draw everyone out, and to encourage every person to participate. We can see an awakening at the grass roots, in every man, woman, and child, no matter what age, stage, background, class, or colour.

Where we have raised up leaders into high places, believing they are the answer to every problem, we have only set them up to fall. Where we have assumed that paid ministers and church buildings and Sunday services is what church is about, we need to re-examine our worldview. Yes, the Lord graciously uses all these things, but there is no evidence of them in Acts, and they can become excuses for observing and not participating in the mission of the kingdom.

Where there is a greater focus on teachers and pastors at the expense of evangelists, apostles, and prophets, we have a problem. What we affirm and value can put 'church' in a box. The Holy Spirit wants to break it out and bring freedom and fulfilment to every single soul in every single gifting. As Ephesians 4:11-12 says, 'So Christ himself gave the apostles, the prophets, the evangelists, the pastors and teachers, to equip his people for works of service, so that the body of Christ may be built up'.

It is fair to say that we probably all know who the shepherds and teachers are in our churches—in many cases they are the paid leaders—but we are challenged to think about who we could name as the evangelists, apostles, and prophets, and if we can each think of them now as we write, do they get recognized in those roles, not just in the church but in the workplace and on the street? Maybe the staff are doing all of the ministries by themselves. Alan Hirsch writes and ministers powerfully relating to the Ephesians 4 ministries. Hirsch writes challenging words: 'The historical reduction of ministry down from the fivefold ministry of the New Testament to that of Christendom's twofold function of shepherding and teaching has bequeathed a fatal and degenerative dis-ease into the body of Christ.'[14] Different Christians have various views of how to categorise these ministries and what exactly they should look like in practice today. But we hope we can all agree that everyone should participate and use their unique gifts in the life of the church.

In Acts, Everyone Acts

They are participators, not observers. Father forgive us for when we have not encouraged folk forward, laid hands on them, and set them apart in every context. Lord, enable us to recognise who carries what and to call it out in them. Lord, help us to re-order our structures to let people flourish. We speak this directly to ourselves as ordained Baptist ministers. Lord, begin with us.

One final note from Hirsch: 'All five functions are needed so that the body of Christ might be perfected, healed, restored, and that it might self-generate, heal, grow and develop. The activation and engagement of the fivefold is not just vital for the mission of the church in the west, but signals renewal of the whole life of the church.'

We can almost hear the voice saying, 'But you cannot pay everyone to operate in every gift. What will you do?' This is one of the biggest problems that we have. Whole livelihoods are built around the shepherding role, so to recognize every person, do we have to provide houses, salaries, and pensions for all of them? And herein lies one of our biggest stumbling blocks in the western church. These questions would never have been in the minds of those first Christians at Antioch because everyone shared everything, and everyone released each other and supported each other like family. We are a long way from there, but God loves his people and is graciously using whatever gifts are laid at his door, paid or not. He is recognizing and releasing his children across the nation. Perhaps the place to start is laying hands on people and praying (Acts 6:7), then seeing the word of God spread (6:8).

Yes, but How?

For you:

Extending our prophetic imagination

The Lord wants to extend our prophetic imaginations as to what he can do in our communities and us. We were both blown away to hear recently from a guy in prison who has been watching our TV show on TBN UK, *Game Changers*, and as a result has been inspired to share his faith in prison and has led lots of the wing to Jesus. We never imagined when filming shows in a studio in Neasden that the Lord could do this with that small offering. What might the Lord do with you if you were prepared to offer what you have?

1 What can you start doing to reach others?
2 How might things be different for you going forward?
3 Do you believe the Lord could multiply your offering significantly for the kingdom?

For your group:

- Have you witnessed a greater emphasis on one age group in the church? Are there generations who might be a little bit overlooked?
- Share with one another the age or group of people that you feel passionate about. How are you seeking to serve and reach them?
- Is hierarchy an issue in your church setting? How might we move towards everybody's role being treated equally?
- Are prophets, apostles, and evangelists affirmed alongside pastors and teachers in your church?
- Who is God calling you to call out of the shadows?

Further Reading:

A. Hirsch, *5Qs* (100 movements, 2017)

The [Im]possible Dream: One People Commission Resource Book (London: Evangelical Alliance, 2019)

S. Clifford, *One* (Oxford: Monarch Books, 2017)

6

Playing Your Part

'All the world's a stage, and all the men and women merely players;
they have their exits and their entrances, and one man in his time
plays many parts.'

William Shakespeare

Our Frontlines

When we first met Mark Greene, we were studying under him at the London School of Theology and were impacted by his unwavering passion for sharing his faith in the secular workplace. This passion of his has developed further during his work at the London Institute for Contemporary Christianity, into the idea of being released to be a Good News person in the places where we spend most of our time. Here he writes:

It's not obviously the most promising context for mission —being a prisoner on a ship that you know is going to sink. But we don't always get to choose our circumstances, and we perhaps don't always see the opportunities for mission in our circumstances, in the places we naturally spend time—work, school, university, the gym, the school gate . . . But in Acts 27, we get a sense of the potential scope of our ministry out in God's world. Paul is under guard on his way to appear before Caesar. So far in Acts we've usually seen Paul in short encounters with people—in the marketplace, speaking on Mars Hill—but here he is in a ship for a prolonged period of time, as many of us are at work, at school, in our families. And he's with 273 people who don't know Jesus.

So how does Paul minister?

He builds a good relationship with the centurion, and so the centurion gives him leave to spend time with his friends in Sidon. He gives the centurion, the pilot, and the ship's owner a clear warning from God about their voyage: if you sail on, the ship will sink. They ignore him. Wisdom from above is not always accepted. So they set sail, the storm comes, and it rages for fourteen days. They throw the cargo and the tackle overboard and everyone despairs for life.

So what does Paul do?

He prays for their physical rescue, not just their eternal salvation. He encourages them emotionally by telling them that not one of them is going to die. He witnesses clearly by telling them that an angel of the God he serves has told him that God has answered his prayer to spare their lives. He strengthens them physically by pushing them to eat because they will need their strength. He protects them practically so that when the crew try to leave, he warns the centurion to stop them.

That's ministry: seeking the best for the people we meet and the organisations we're involved with, offering wisdom from above, praying for physical protection, testifying to what God does, and taking prayerful, practical initiatives for the physical, emotional, and spiritual welfare of those around us. And trusting the living God to do what only he can do.

But what happens if Paul is not on that ship? Maybe it sinks. Maybe everyone drowns.

And what happens if you're not on your frontline—your workplace, your gym, your school? Maybe the sick colleague doesn't get prayed for, maybe the contract doesn't come in, maybe your school friend fails their exam? You may not be in your dream job, on your dream street, on your dream town, but while you are where you are, God has a role for you.

For every one of us there are places and people with whom we find ourselves able to make a difference. We are uniquely placed to make a difference for the kingdom. In his book *Fruitfulness on the Frontline,* Mark also talks about six M's that provide a framework for fruitfulness. These are: (1) Modelling godly character, (2) Making good work, (3) Ministering grace and love, (4) Moulding culture, (5) being a Mouthpiece for truth and justice, and (6) being a Messenger of the gospel.[1] These six things lived out properly make a huge difference, not just to the workplace, but also to the family, sports team, social club, etc. All of us can do each of these six things and bring about change in the environments we find ourselves in. On our frontlines. We cannot rely on the gathered church to change the nation; it's when we are all released into our everyday environments that real differences can take place.

One Young Person

For some of us, the best thing to do is to simply stop and listen to the Lord's heart. What might he be challenging you to do? What might the Lord have for us that's right in front of us? What is there that might need to be done to make a difference? What is going on right where we are? When the Lord turns the tables in Luke 19, it is because the poor are being exploited financially as they seek to bring an act of worship to the temple. Jesus sees that something is wrong, and it needs changing. The rest of the people miss it. Sometimes our culture blinds us to what needs to change, and we need to ask the Lord to see things as he does. When we seek the Jesus way, then things have to change. Michael Wilcock puts it this way in relation to the cleansing of the temple and our own lives: 'We may all find, as Jesus enters our own "temple" and inspects our faith and life, things that need to be thoroughly cleaned out from it.'[2]

There are always things that need to change, and we need to ask the Lord what some of these are. Mark Pugh leads a church down in

Exeter. In his congregation is a teenage girl who last winter was really upset about the amount of homelessness in the wider community. She knew that this was not okay, and righteous anger burnt in her to make a difference as she saw the homeless as Jesus saw them. Driven into action, she appealed to the church to buy hot water bottles to help homeless people stay warm in the name of Jesus. She got over 100 sponsored hot water bottles from the congregation, and then convinced businesses throughout the city to fill them up at the end of each day with hot water for the homeless to then collect, to help them get through the night ahead. Then in the morning, each hot water bottle is returned to that business in order to be filled again for the following night. That is what it means to be an unleashed church.

How many of us see the growing problem of homelessness and just think it's too big to fix? I, Gavin, work in Kings Cross where the problem has become noticeably worse in recent times. How often it feels like there's nothing that can be done to make much of an impact, and yet the story of this teenage girl shows that an impact can really be made when we act on what we are feeling from the Lord. It reminds us of the old story of the starfish on the beach. We can't do everything at once, but we can always make a difference. Here's that famous old story.

One day, an old man was walking along a beach that was littered with thousands of starfish that had been washed ashore by the high tide. As he walked he came upon a young boy who was eagerly throwing the starfish back into the ocean, one by one.

Puzzled, the man looked at the boy and asked what he was doing. Without looking up from his task, the boy simply replied, "I'm saving these starfish, Sir."

The old man chuckled aloud, "Son, there are thousands of starfish and only one of you. What difference can you make?"

The boy picked up a starfish, gently tossed it into the water and turning to the man, said, "I made a difference to that one![3]

An unleashed church follows the example of Jesus. It cares about each and every person, leaving the ninety-nine to help the one (Luke 15).

Anointed

Let us just remember for a second that the teachers of the law identified the apostles as 'Unschooled, ordinary men' (Acts 4:13). These early believers were normal people empowered and emboldened by the Spirit of the Living God, doing and saying what they felt led to do and say. When the Holy Spirit gets hold of people, what they would be naturally gifted in gets added to, changes, and is anointed to a different level. We no longer just work together in a 'natural' way but in a 'supernatural' one. Look at Stephen, one of the Seven chosen to wait on tables (6:5)—clearly a practical, wise man. However, he is also described as 'a man full of God's grace and power who did great wonders and signs among the people.' Where did that come from? He was also the man who stood, boldly proclaimed the gospel to the Sanhedrin with authority they couldn't stand up to (6:10), and the face of an angel (6:15). To box Stephen as a waiter at tables and conclude that his role was limited to one space might never have unleashed him into all those other gifts and places. 'You never know, once you lay hands on people and pray for God to work through them, what new things they will get up to, or rather, what new things God will do through them!'[4]

God takes our simple lives and blows through them by the wind of his Spirit to release kingdom gifts that when brought together with others,' will change the world. We think of the incredible treasurer at our church, who is amazing at handling finances but in the last couple of years has found herself working with a charity to help prostitutes on the streets of London—this was not a natural decision, but rather a move of the Spirit in her life. We think of our friend ordering Bibles in Farsi for our church, believing that the Spirit had led her to do it because 'Iranians were coming' she declared. Two weeks later when I, Anne, was preaching a message about Iranians in solitary confinement and God moving through them in power, an Iranian man with no faith felt led to get in his car a mile away, drive past one church and then pull over and park outside ours, coming in as we were talking about his people. At the end of the service we chatted, and my friend presented him with a Bible in his own language. The Holy Spirit was at work in a way that was way beyond our imagination. He has recently gotten saved and baptized. Praise Jesus! What strikes us the most is that God was using our gifts together in a supernatural way. There is so much more he longs to do. Laying hands on the Seven, praying, delegating, releasing, and empowering the people grew the church and united the people. The question is, are we doing it?

To All Our Friends

We are carriers of the gospel, and it's vital that we share that with those around us however challenging that may seem. Encouragingly, a few years ago when it felt that a new atheism, spearheaded by the likes of Richard Dawkins, might be having a huge resurgence, there are actually fewer atheists in the world today (138 million) than there were in 1970 (165 million). Atheism is expected to decline again and fall below 130 million by 2050.[5] At the same time, Christianity is growing rapidly all over the globe, and we in the UK need to play our part in this. The absolute best way for us to do so is one-to-one—through our conversations, lives, and relationships.

Our friend Phil Knox lives for peer-to-peer evangelism and writes about it this way:

2014 saw an outbreak of the Ebola virus that tragically killed many people, especially in West Africa. The BBC reported the potential threat to the UK at the time and stated that, 'The Department of Health said a man had been tested for Ebola in

Birmingham but tests for the virus had proved negative.' When my friend sent me the article, I immediately knew this [to be true], because the man in question was me.

I had been abroad and arrived home with the worst flu I had ever experienced. Upon mentioning to the doctor that I had been with colleagues from Sierra Leone, I was immediately quarantined, wearing a mask, with a biohazard symbol on my hospital door, feeling like the star of an apocalyptic disaster movie. I was contained by people who know the power of contagiousness.

As Christians, we have in our heart and in our hands the most contagious message of hope the world has ever known. The good news of Jesus spreads quickest and most effectively from contagious Christians to the people they are closest to.

We see this throughout the book of Acts. The beautiful message of the life-transforming power of Jesus captivates people and rapidly spreads through families and communities. Take Lydia for example in Acts 16. Paul and his team of evangelists touch down in the city of Philippi and meet a businesswoman, a dealer in purple cloth. Paul tells her about Jesus, the Holy Spirit opens her heart, and she joins the ever-growing movement of Christ-followers. But you get the feeling that Lydia instinctively knows this message is not just for her, and we read that her whole household are baptized. The first thing that happens to her after she becomes a Christian is that she is unleashed on those around her. It is her household, those closest to her that are impacted first.

Just about the next time we encounter Philippi in the Bible is a letter from Paul to the Philippians. By the time this letter is written, there is a thriving, growing church there. The Gospel is exploding, lives are being changed, and it started with one person, an ordinary clothing entrepreneur telling her closest contacts.

We are not all called to be a nomadic church-planting, gospel preacher like Paul. But we are all called to be like Lydia: a contagious example of Jesus to those around us who care enough about our friends and family to pray for them and take opportunities to tell our story and invite them to hear and experience the most important message in the world. This is rarely easy, but we do need to try.

Callings Connecting

Imagine if we all began to move in the individual callings that God has empowered us to minister in—side by side, serving Jesus with all that the Spirit has equipped us to do. It is amazing to discover what we are called to do in service for the King and work out our own unique contribution, but when that comes alongside someone else who has worked out theirs, the body of Christ truly begins to move together.

The apostles slowly began to work out where they were each called to fly. Some were meant to travel, others were to oversee those who were being overlooked, many preached, others prayed, some taught, some healed, etc. Some of them did all of the above, and others moved from role to role depending on the season or who they encountered that day and how the Holy Spirit was leading them.

The Lord might call you like Lydia, Paul, Stephen, or Barnabas, but who is he putting alongside you? We see very little 'independent' ministry going on in Acts. Even when Paul and Barnabas quarrel, they do not continue alone.

We may have a vision of connecting with preschool parents, serving tea and coffee, building relationships, praying for them, and running Alpha amongst them, but this vision is not a 'one person' job. If the Lord is calling you to something, he will provide all you need for his plans to prevail.

The Fight to Be One

We know that Acts is clear that being the body of Christ, as Paul talks about in 1 Corinthians 12 and being 'One as We are One' as Jesus prays in John 17 is a powerful draw for the lost and vital for fulfilling the Great Commission effectively. However, it is one of the biggest challenges for the church today. How can we really see 'one heart and mind' worked out, the sharing of possessions, the every-day connection, the level of fellowship displayed in Acts right here and now in the UK?

We live in North-west London where our fight for 'togetherness' is against the rush of commuters, the pull of devices, the craziness of family life, the running of the home, the consumer mentality, and so much more. It is very difficult to establish a body mentality in church when there are so many distractions. As we have begun to pray and long for a move of the Spirit in our neighbourhood and in our land, it has been interesting to see how Jesus is bringing his people together. Where there is a will, there is a way.

Think about the backdrop of Acts

They were living in the midst of opposition, of persecution, and a few things happened as a result of that. There were constant threats, imprisonment, Stephen is stoned to death—the list goes on. Through all of these difficulties, the church pull together and pray and serve and worship—they love one another. Togetherness can come about on a whole new level through tough times.

Instead of just changing our diaries so that we can make space to meet together, the Lord has begun, where we are, to bring us together through an increased amount of challenges. In the last year, growing numbers of folk in the church have been poorly, hospitalized, fallen down, or been suffering in some way. It has been so hard having so many people in distress, but something amazing has happened too: prayer has increased, care has increased, unity has grown.

You can never write a book and not live the words because it would make the narrative fake. We long to see the Holy Spirit move, togetherness increase, and to look, sound, and do more of what the Lord is calling us to do: to be like the early church. However, we can sometimes forget that there is a fight on now as much as there was then.

The Lord is teaching his church to come together as one through engaging weapons of sacrificial love and prayer. He is equipping his army for a mighty move of his Spirit, and if we are going to be ready to ride the wave, we need to pull together in the face of opposition and declare who we are in him. To really begin to step into Acts 2, we need to love one another in a way that goes against the cultural narrative and infectiously draws the lost towards the King.

Yes, but How?

For you:

Your Frontline

How can you take Mark Greene's six M's and apply them to your frontline? What do each of them mean for your context? (1) Modelling godly character, (2) Making good work, (3) Ministering grace and love, (4) Moulding culture, (5) being a Mouthpiece for truth and justice, and (6) being a Messenger of the gospel.

To All Our Friends

Here are three things we can do to be more contagious and unleashed amongst our friends:

- Pray for them. Make a list of a few friends or family to pray for regularly to come to faith.
- Know your story. Most people break into a cold sweat at the thought of a conversation about faith. The best starting point is to know and practice telling your story of why you follow Jesus.
- Have a go! More people than we think are interested in being invited to church. Choose the type of service or event carefully and then go for it. And if they say no or make an excuse, pick yourself up, dust yourself down, and keep praying.

For your group:

- Share together the passions of your heart—what you really want to see.
- Call out the gold in one another—begin to tell each other what gifts and passions you see in each other. Encourage each other to have a go.
- Ask each other to identify who is alongside you with a similar heart but different gifts.

- Who could gather with you to minister more effectively together? It may be that some could pray, serve coffee, help you raise funds, or the profile.
- Pray for one another that together you could unleash God's dreams through your lives.

LICC

LICC may well have the resources to help you make the most of the opportunities to serve, to bless, to show and share the gospel out in your bit of God's world. Check out licc.org.uk for a trove of biblically rich, culturally astute resources, films, books, and prayer-journeys for individuals and groups, church leaders and teams, as well as a range of courses, learning hubs and training days—all designed to help you make a difference right where you are. Find at more at www.licc.org.uk.

Further Reading

M. Greene, *Fruitfulness on the Frontline* (Nottingham: IVP, 2014)
S. Dendy, *Simply Church* (Farnham: CWR, 2020)
P. Knox, *Story Bearer* (London: IVP, 2020)

7

Ministering Together

Frodo: 'Go back, Sam. I'm going to Mordor alone.'
Sam: 'Of course you are. And I'm coming with you.'

Taken from *The Lord of the Rings:*
***The Fellowship of the Ring*[1] by J. R. R. Tolkien**

As local church commitments began to increase for me, Anne, in an urban deprived area of the West Midlands, we were dreaming of what it would look like to build church in the way the Holy Spirit was leading. One woman had been faithfully serving Jesus for years, running Alpha groups for women, ministering to those mums who had postpartum depression, and taking furniture and food around the neighbourhood to families in need. Now the Lord was awakening the leadership to what was already happening and calling us to push in further to see the fullness of her heart released and to hear God's heart over his vision for the whole body. The leader I was ministering with suggested I pen a preaching series on the book of Acts, and I readily agreed.

As a leadership team we began to press in with prayer, seeking to discern where the Lord was leading, alongside preaching and activating the acts of the apostles. I remember so clearly a dream I had during that time. We were witnessing the Holy Spirit begin to unlock callings and unearth leaders. Looking back, there was a wider move of God's mission that, like a wave was moving through our church, and we were doing our best to ride it.

One night I dreamt that I was leading a service at the church and during worship I invited people to come forward with what they had brought with them. My sense was that we had asked them to pray during the week and ask God what he wanted them to bring, then they came to the service carrying whatever it was. As the people came forward with their offering of worship, I noticed lots of different items were being placed at the front: some money, a baby rocker, a DVD, a voucher for electricity, an item of clothing, etc. Then we paused, continued in worship, and I asked people to pray and come forward to receive what they needed. Every single item was something that an individual not only needed, but also had prayed for. Through this ministry, people were feeling part of the body, blessing one another, hearing and responding to the call of God, and it was attracting people to God's church.

When I awoke from the dream, I felt a real excitement come over me. What would it look like to activate something like that? What was amazing was that the Lord was also at work in others at the same time (Don't you just love how he does that?): my friend was starting to fill her car with items that people needed and drive them around the neighbourhood, providing for those in need. The Holy Spirit was speaking clearly to her through the Acts narrative too, and her heart was broken over what she had and what they didn't have.

A real dream began to unfold through this season. The woman who was already ministering to so many women and families preached a message that enacted the dream, we started using cards that said: 'I can give…' on one side, and 'I need….' on the other. These two women began to lead and birth the ministry Acts4Needs. Gifts were brought to the church and laid at the front to one side, and people from the community were able to come and receive what they needed. Alongside this ministry we served breakfast, continued to run Alpha, Bible studies, freedom in Christ, and a group for mums suffering with postpartum depression. More volunteers came forward, and their gifts were utilized. The gospel was at work in a full and exciting way, and it was so incredible watching God at work as we ministered together out of what he was clearly calling us to do.

Now I watch from afar with a huge smile because Acts4Needs

grew into a CAP (Christians Against Poverty) centre run by my friend, a coffee shop that ministers to so many, and the gifts are still being shared amongst those in need. When we begin to pray and invite the Holy Spirit and his agenda, incredible things begin to unfold, not just in one of us but also in the whole team.

Receivers Becoming Servers

Another challenge comes to us as we consider the Acts4needs ministry ministering to those who are struggling and the early church in Acts giving to those in need. At some point in this 'togetherness' narrative that the Lord longs to unleash through his church, we have to engage the receivers. We are called to love and serve one another, but at some point the congregation are called to participate too. This is not just 'us' helping 'them,' but 'them' helping 'us' and 'others' as well. As Francis Chan has explored reimagining church to look more as God might long for it to look, he deliberately 'decided to find the most overlooked in our congregation to remind them of Biblical truth and tell them how badly we needed them.'[2] Whether they are struggling because of being overlooked, poor, weak, old, or any other reason, does not mean they are relegated from the fivefold or not a key part of the unfolding mission of God. One of our greatest prophets is in her 80s, and her words steer our body in the most profound ways.

God uses the prophets, the teachers, the shepherds, the evangelists, and the apostles all together to reach the people and spread the gospel. There is a powerful moment in Acts where the prophets come down from Jerusalem to Antioch, and Agabus prophesies to the people there that a severe famine would spread over the entire Roman world. As a response to this, the disciples, 'each according to his ability', decided to provide help for the brothers living in Judea. This they did, sending their gift to the elders by Barnabas and Saul (the famine comes during the reign of Claudius;

Acts 11:27-30). Here is another moment when the people of God utilize their gifts and their resources together to love and support one another in the days ahead. They don't just listen to the prophet and hope someone else will do something about it or shove aside the word, they actively ask what they can do and then do it. James Montgomery Boice writes: 'As far as I know this is the first charitable act of this nature in all recorded history—one race of people collecting money to help another people.' He also notes that when hearing Agabus, 'they being full of the Holy Spirit of Christ, immediately asked what Christ, would do in such a situation.'[3] What would Jesus do? There it is, that famous saying that really does transform lives when we ask and respond to it together.

When we gather together and display our gifts, networking, ministering, and discussions together, new dreams and callings are birthed. Our friend Anne's daughter, Abi, talks about how growing up in the summer conference atmosphere led her to sponsor a child in Colombia, then go on a mission trip to Colombia, and eventually become a missionary there. She says: 'All those contacts from the exhibition area, and my passion to serve in the kingdom of God, came from years of spiritual formation and [the] living examples I saw modelled in the youth groups and leadership.'[4] In our 'togetherness', life becomes vibrant and the Holy Spirit uses it to unlock his purposes. Imagine having the eyes to see what the Lord can see as all over the world he is connecting people, joining the missional dots, in order to fulfil his purposes. Some of the togetherness is happening in the towns and villages, some of it crosses into other boroughs, and other ministries span countries and continents.

Help All People

Tim Morfin is the founder of Transforming Lives for Good (TGL), a Christian charity that helps churches bring hope and a future to struggling children and their families. He writes:

The email inbox of TLG has never been so busy! It seems there's a heart for mission and ministry to struggling children like never before. Be it food for children who are hungry in the holidays, one-to-one Early Intervention for kids struggling in school, or education for young people who've blown it in mainstream school. Churches are rising up to meet these needs at a rate I've never seen before, unleashing love and compassion in enormous quantities with dramatic 'early church' effect.

TLG is just one of many ministries equipping churches to consistently reach and serve their communities. [through] Foodbanks, debt counseling help, and housing for people at risk of being homeless. Increasingly in our society the church is the place where the best help is given, and life transformation happens.

The early disciples followed the example of Jesus in the outworking of a practical gospel of mercy and compassion. In Acts 3 v 6, Peter, who had no silver or gold with him, gave a crippled beggar what he did have: the gift of health and wholeness.

What's our response when we encounter those crippled by the circumstances of their lives? I was a volunteer in my twenties when I joined a church in inner-city Bradford West Yorkshire. We opened a youth club and a whole crowd of kids came along. I first met Lewis when he was twelve; he punched me. That was Lewis's way of introducing himself to most people! [His] Periods of attendance at school were, at best, short-lived. Exclusions, typically the result of fighting, resulted in months of missed education. Lewis hardly ever made it to the end of a school day and had no other routine in his life; yet every time we opened the youth club or had a church meeting, Lewis was there.

By the age of fifteen, Lewis had entirely stopped going to school and we realized we had to do something. Having got to know his mum well over the preceding few years, we worked together to ask if we could spend time coaching and supporting him, alongside attendance at school. Help for the school with one of their most challenging students turned out to be an offer they couldn't refuse!

TLG now supports church volunteers to get alongside struggling children through a one-to-one coaching programme in school, and provides food for children on Free School Meals who are at risk of [experiencing] hunger in the holidays. Through a fast-growing network of more than 250 churches, TLG is now directly supporting more than 6,000 children each year, bringing life-transforming help, and connecting struggling families into the wider support of a local church.

I'm sure you're wondering what happened to Lewis. Where is he now? Lewis is now a man in his thirties, who says that without that help, he'd be in prison or dead. He works as a groundsman, has his own faith, and is passionate about children getting the help they need when life is tough.

Obviously, things don't always end this well, and the journey in relationships can be really challenging, but it's incredible when we see such breakthroughs.

Division

We are very grateful that it is not all just plain sailing in Acts, and all the believers are not best friends all the time. Yes, we read of them all joining together constantly in prayer, and yes, we hear of them sharing their possessions and meeting every day, but we also stumble across a disagreement and a breakdown in relationship between Paul and Barnabas. In Acts 13:2-3, when the two of them are clearly set apart by the Holy Spirit, the believers lay their hands on them and send them off. This is a God thing: the relationship, the calling, everything. And yet by Acts 15, we encounter a problem. Paul and

Barnabas have been ministering effectively together and yet they disagree about who will travel with them: Barnabas wants to take John (also called Mark), but Paul does not because John had deserted them. The argument is so severe that they part ways (15:36-41).

Let's note, too, that these two don't obviously reconcile at any point. They carry on ministering but they do it separately, and we hear much more of Paul's story as we move ahead. We are all human, and there will be disagreements and troubles in our relationships as we seek to be one body ministering in his name wherever we find ourselves. There are seasons when the body does not work well together, and the challenge is not to shove these issues under the carpet and continue as normal because that's exactly what the enemy wants us to do.

If the Lord longs to display his glory through our unity, you can be certain that the enemy will seek to steal, kill, and destroy it. We believe that the Lord is calling us to be honest with what is really going on in our relationships with one another, to begin to speak openly, to forgive quickly, and to keep loving even when it hurts. If we are not for one another in the church, how can we ever expect other people to see anything different in our lives?

It is so sad how much negativity there can be within the church and how one word is like a flicker of a flame that can suddenly erupt and blow up the whole room of people. As our old lecturer at Bible college used to say, 'Little tigers grow into big tigers, and big tigers kill.' One of the most painful challenges we have faced in ministry is so-called 'friendly fire'—the people who are closest to us can often be those who hurt us the most. Wouldn't it be so incredible if we stopped talking about one another in such a negative way? If we forgave all the mistakes our leaders have made? If we began to look for ways to stick together and be for each other like we have never been before?

The pastor and teacher Craig Groeshel says, 'Often the loudest boos come from the cheapest seats'[5] in relation to our congregations. Booing is surely reserved for a bad performance in the theatre or in sports, not amongst a church body who are all seeking to serve alongside one another. What we do with our tongue has the potential to quickly disrupt a move of the Spirit of God, not only deeply damaging us but also everyone around us: 'The tongue is a small part of the body, but it makes great boasts. Consider what a great forest is set on fire by a small spark. . . no man can tame the tongue. It is a restless evil full of deadly poison' (James 3:5,8). We are not perfect, far from it, but the power of the Holy Spirit can help us to keep working together, loving one another, and being for one another.

If there is something causing deep relational trouble amongst the people of God, then it has to be dealt with. We must not let wolves run around in sheep's clothing. Groeshel talks about how sickness is contagious and we need to remove the sickness from the room or it will pass to others and make everyone poorly. Sometimes we have to address an issue with a person—we need to endure the pain of surgery to take out what needs cutting away. The whole body cannot grow up healthily, powerfully, and effectively if one part is working its sickness through the rest. None of this is easy, but growth of any type is painful, and when it is dealt with we will say, 'I wish we had done that a long time ago!'[6]

We are not suggesting naming and shaming people in public, or accusing folk without evidence. It is about soaking our words in prayer, speaking the truth in love, face-to-face, and suggesting a way ahead. Sometimes, like Paul and Barnabas, we may have to go separate ways; the longing is that it is done in peace and with reconciliation. We are all on that journey. Let's seek to reverse the tide of negativity and unkindness, and work to see lives transformed by the power of God together, uniting over what we are for, rather than dividing over what we are against. As the church we have a chance to show the world true unity when the nation often feels divided. There is often a negative script lived out in culture where people unite in fear over what they're against and adopt a common enemy or scapegoat. As the church, let's live in contrast to this with a hopeful script, knowing the grave is empty, that we can be one in Christ and that the church is plan A for changing the world.

Yes, but How?

For you:

- Is there anyone in your life who has recently caused you pain? Have you dealt with it?
- Has hurt ever limited you from forgiving or moving forward?
- The enemy would like to convince you that it is better to hold onto the pain. However, Jesus longs for you to be honest with him and to allow him to bring healing.

For your group:

- Who ministers alongside you?
- Do you see the gifts that you have complementing, and being complemented by, others around you? If so, how?
- Is there anyone else that God might want to use in what you are seeking to do?
- Why not pray that the Lord would show you how to minister together more, and invite his spirit to knit your gifts together to accomplish great things.

Personality tests

Myers Briggs:
http://www.myersbriggs.org/my-mbti-personality-type/take-the-mbti-instrument/

Gallup strengths finder:
https://www.gallupstrengthscenter.com/?utm_source=googadwords&utm_medium=web&utm_campaign=newhomepage&gclid=CKfav5yZxsYCFQoYwwodVYcNpA

What is your SHAPE?

Take a moment to consider your 'SHAPE' (Spiritual Gifts, Heart, Abilities, Personality, Experience). List what you think your three key things are under each heading. Are you currently making use of them all? Consider how any neglected features could be used. Consider the same for others around you.

Helping you make a difference:

There are loads of Christian ministries out there that can help you make a difference. From looking after the environment to helping people in debt, from transforming our communities to working with young people, from working on the streets of your town to providing for the neediest on the planet, the ways to get involved are many.

To search a list of hundreds of organizations that are keen to have you involved, go to: https://www.eauk.org/membership/our-members /find-an-organisation.

Further Reading:

M. Buckingham, *Now Discover Your Strengths* (London: Pocket Books, 2004)

B. Bugbee, *What You Do Best in the Body of Christ* (Grand Rapids: Zondervan, 2005)

Part 3

UNLEASHED PRESENCE

Acts 5:12–25

Acts 5:12-25

The Apostles Heal Many

The apostles performed many signs and wonders among the people. And all the believers used to meet together in Solomon's Colonnade. [13]No one else dared join them, even though they were highly regarded by the people. [14]Nevertheless, more and more men and women believed in the Lord and were added to their number. [15]As a result, people brought the sick into the streets and laid them on beds and mats so that at least Peter's shadow might fall on some of them as he passed by. [16]Crowds gathered also from the towns around Jerusalem, bringing their sick and those tormented by impure spirits, and all of them were healed.

The Apostles Persecuted

[17]Then the high priest and all his associates, who were members of the party of the Sadducees, were filled with jealousy. [18]They arrested the apostles and put them in the public jail. [19]But during the night an angel of the Lord opened the doors of the jail and brought them out. [20]"Go, stand in the temple courts," he said, "and tell the people all about this new life."

[21]At daybreak they entered the temple courts, as they had been told, and began to teach the people.

When the high priest and his associates arrived, they called together the Sanhedrin—the full assembly of the elders of Israel—and sent to the jail for the apostles. [22]But on arriving at the jail, the officers did not find them there. So they went back and reported, [23]"We found the jail securely locked, with the guards standing at the doors; but when we opened them, we found no one inside." [24]On hearing this report, the captain of the temple guard and the chief priests were at a loss, wondering what this might lead to.

[25]Then someone came and said, "Look! The men you put in jail are standing in the temple courts teaching the people."

8

Empowered to Share

'Movements begin with white-hot faith.'

Steve Addison

So much of Acts is about how to share the gospel in a challenging environment. In fact, the book of 'Acts tells the exciting story of how the Spirit led the early Jesus community to respond creatively and continually in new and surprising situations as it preached the gospel.'[1] The early church are constantly looking for opportunities. In Acts 4:18-19, they simply cannot help but speak about Jesus. They were effectively being tried under the charge of being Christians. Throughout the history of the church, somewhere in the world, someone has been tried for the same charge. This gospel poured out of the early Christians as naturally as sweat from an athlete's brow. Moving on to Acts 5, there is a particularly exciting passage (verses 12-25) that shows the impact of sharing the gospel and the cost of this on the early church.

Our God is All-Powerful (Acts 5:12-16)

We are both keen runners. We love the freedom of running outside and the space it provides in our busy lives for a bit of quiet and some time alone with the Lord. When we both run, we do so in Adidas running shoes. There are obviously many other choices, but due to there being an outlet store of that particular brand near our house, these are the shoes for us. Adidas has a simple, but powerful, advertising slogan: 'Impossible is nothing.' Every time either of us put our feet in our running shoes, this proves to be false marketing. Much is impossible for us as runners, now matter how hard we try or train.

In Acts 5, it is the fact that God is doing things that gets the apostles in trouble again. Unlike our running, with God, absolutely nothing is impossible. He is truly all-powerful. We instinctively know this, but it certainly helps to be reminded of the fact that nothing is beyond him. We like to sing of him moving mountains, and truly he could do so in a moment in our communities. We must do all we can to avoid the trap of minimizing the Lord's power or making him small enough that we find him palatable. There is literally nothing beyond the power of Jesus.

At this point in the book of Acts, the church's activities were increasing to such an extent that the authorities needed to take action against it.[2] Angered by the failure of their first assault on the apostles, dismayed to see that they had ignored the court's threats, and filled with jealousy of the apostles' power and popularity, the High Priest and all his associates resolve to take further action. This anger provoked the second attack by the authorities, much as the healing of the cripple had provoked the first. In this passage we see words, works, and wonders all coming together. Having previously given a verbal account of their message, here we see a description of the extraordinary signs (works and wonders combined) that authenticated the words.[3]

The power of God is such a reassurance to us as we seek to do things in his name. This means that even when we do things badly, it's important to remember that he's so powerful that he can still use us profoundly. I, Gavin, preached my worst-ever sermon a little over a decade ago. I was invited to speak on a Friday night at a youth event in North Wales. I set off on what felt like the longest-ever journey and finally pulled into the coastal location I was heading to. I'd been told there would be hundreds of young people there, but as the event started, I realized I have more fingers than there were young people there. In total, only nine teenagers had shown up.

The event had been arranged by a bunch of the churches working together across the town, and they had clubbed together to hire in a ten-foot-high stage. As they'd paid for it, they insisted that I preach from it. I'm already 6 ft. 3 in. tall, so there I was, essentially speaking from 16 feet in the air, towering above a bunch of young people significantly smaller in number than the disciples. I didn't want to be there, but I had been invited for a purpose. Therefore, I preached the gospel as expected but, if I'm honest, I did it pretty inadequately and was in a bad mood.

When my evening there was over, I was handed an envelope. Back in the day before bank transfers, you used to operate in the 'ministry of envelopes'. You'd be given one with a cheque in it towards your ministry. I never opened the envelope till I got home as I always felt it was for the Lord and me to discuss how an event had gone, not for me to be influenced either way by the figure on the cheque. As I finally arrived home in the early hours of the next morning, I opened the envelope and out fell the ministry gift: a £5 book token. You can't put that in the petrol tank. I'd paid for the privilege of what felt like my worst sermon ever, and I was not pleased.

Ten years later, I was preaching in the north of England. After one event, a guy in his mid-twenties came up to me and started describing the disastrous youth event. I wondered how he knew about it when he suddenly said, 'I gave my life to Jesus that night.' Frankly, I was flabbergasted. How was that even possible with how that evening had gone? He then continued to tell me that he was now a Christian youth worker and had recently done an outreach event on a local estate and thirty-two young lads had given their lives to Jesus. As I drove home that night, I was utterly overjoyed and thanked the Lord that sometimes, even when we are inadequate, you still only have to impact one Samaritan woman to reach a village. Our God is all-powerful! Nothing is beyond him.

Once people have met him they see how wonderful, powerful, and majestic he is, they also start to see themselves in the right way.

The American theologian, R. C. Sproul puts it this way: 'Men are never duly touched and impressed with a conviction of their insignificance, until they have contrasted themselves with the majesty of God.'[4] This all-powerful God changes everything!

Christianity Can't Be Swept Away (Acts 5:17-21a)

The open defiance of the Sanhedrin's ban on preaching in public, coupled with the success of their outreach, led to this second arrest of the apostles.[5] This time it is not only Peter and John who were arrested, but also the rest of apostles. Most, if not all of them, were thrown into a public jail. But during the night, they were rescued by an angel of the Lord who instructed them to publicly proclaim the message of this new life.[6] Wow, what a risk! The whole passage here is remarkable. The authorities think that by locking up the Christians the problem is dealt with. So often, society thinks it can get be rid of Christianity fairly simply, but this is impossible.

Throughout the history of the church people have thought that they can wipe Christianity out by pressurizing and persecuting it—from Emperor Nero dipping some of the early followers in pitch and using them as human candles in his garden to the so-called Islamic State of recent times, many have tried to get rid of the church. Individual Christians have been martyred and persecuted, but the church remains and will never be wiped away. Remarkably, too, as the church is really persecuted, it grows at a far greater rate than when it is left alone in freedom. As the early church father Tertullian put it, 'The blood of the martyrs is the seed of the church.'

Christianity never claimed to be an easy ride. James 1 stresses quite the opposite: 'Consider it pure joy, my brothers, whenever you face trials of many kinds, because you know that the testing of your faith develops perseverance' (verses 2-3). The Christian life is tough, but it's well worth it. David Field points us toward the example of Jesus: he spent most of his ministry struggling or under pressure. He had nowhere he could truly call home, he wept by his friend's tomb (John 11), he was constantly being watched and accused of breaking Pharisaical laws (Matthew 12), he felt profound compassion for his people and their needs (Matthew 9:36), he sweated with mental agony in the garden of Gethsemane (Matthew 26), and died in torment on the cross (Matthew 27). Significantly, he also warned his followers that they would not escape the stresses and strains that he himself had to face (Matthew 5).[7]

Some strain is inevitable, and we need to get used to it. In the UK we are certainly not being persecuted, but we are more marginalized than we have been before. There is a growing 'chill factor' towards evangelical Christianity, and we are finding ourselves increasingly on the wrong side of social orthodoxy. As this happens, we need to hold onto the fact that we know the end of the story. No matter how many bad things happen between now and the end of time— however many wars, rumours of wars, famines, murders, and much more, the end is the same. Likewise, however many good things happen— many cures are found for previously incurable illnesses, however many revivals, however many people are liberated from slavery, however many World Cups England wins—still the end remains unchanged. However much good or bad happens between now and the end of time, the end is unchanged. Jesus wins and his church cannot be swept away. Therefore, we must be more confident in our day and face the challenges, pressures, and even persecution that come with this.

This is backed up further later in the passage when Gamaliel (an honoured teacher of the Law) stands up in front of the Sanhedrin and says, 'I advise you leave these men alone! Let them go! For if their purpose or activity is of human origin, it will fail. But if it is from God, you will not be able to stop these men; you will only find your selves fighting against God' (Acts 5:34-39, abbreviated). Who would want to find themselves fighting against the King of Kings? Nothing can stop the power of God. We must not underestimate how a move of the Spirit can override any human physical activity.

We Are Compelled to Share the Message (Acts 5:21b-25)

The Sanhedrin was convened, and they were humiliated to discover on sending for the apostles, that they were no longer in the prison where they had put them. This is one of those moments in Scripture when we would have loved to be flies on the wall in the room. How did the Sanhedrin really respond to this flabbergasting news? The apostles who they had locked up were no longer in their cell. The door was still locked, the bars had not been tampered with, and the guards could not account for their disappearance. The smartly dressed, wealthy Sanhedrin with brains the size of the solar system could not work out between them what had happened. Later, the Sanhedrin would be absolutely furious when they realize that the apostles they had locked up for preaching in public were instead in the temple courts teaching the people as they had been forbidden to do. The words of the apostles, as they preached once more, had to be rooted in the reality of how they were living and the work of the healing they were doing.[8] Again it's all about words, works, and wonders coming together. All these elements must work together. There is no room for the kind of separation in our witnessing that previous generations have accepted. The missiologist Leslie Newbigin puts it this way: 'It is the Word made flesh that is the gospel. The deed without the word is dumb, and the word without the deed is empty.'[9] Add the wonders, and we have the whole picture.

Once we have met the risen Jesus, then we should really find ourselves compelled to share. Good news is designed for sharing, and the gospel is no different. We need to be so in awe of him that we can't help but speak of him. The *Guardian* newspaper was looking at key words in our time and one was 'vegangelical'.[10] This means that someone is so passionate about their veganism that this can't help but impact everyone around them. If that works for veganism in our culture then surely it's equally okay to be the same about the gospel.

It can be really hard to witness and stand out for Jesus, but it's a huge comfort to know that nothing shall ever rob us of his presence. The Gospel of Matthew begins with the promise that this baby to be born would be called 'Immanuel' meaning 'God is with us' (Matthew 1:23). That same gospel closes with the promise, within the Great Commission, that he is with them still, and will be until the end of time (Matthew 28:20).[11] Whatever life currently holds for us, we are not alone and can face it in the comfort and confidence of his unwavering presence.

So here in our world today, we dream of seeing the church reaching out to the UK like never before and beginning to fulfil the Great Commission in our day. This is always directed outwards, to the unreached. It is a call to a discipling, teaching evangelism. Through this, every single location is a sharing location. The cinema, the bank, the school playground, the football terrace, our workplaces are all locations where we live Jesus, show Jesus, talk Jesus, and help others to walk like Jesus.[12]

All of the early church were compelled to share and so are we. Witnessing is not for certain personalities, but for all Christians to share with those that we are uniquely placed amongst. Such ministry must involve words, works, and wonders within it.

One Way to Share

Ben Jack, an evangelist working at *The Message Trust*, writes:

Advance[13] started in 2015 as a method by which experienced evangelists could mentor those who wanted to develop evangelistic gifting. Using a simple group framework of regular meeting, a focus on sharpening each other in the truth of the gospel and the ability to share it, and a commitment to being accountable to one another, these evangelism-focused mentoring groups began to launch around the globe.

As of today there are more than a thousand evangelists being mentored each month through the Advance framework and resources. Some are platform preachers who have regular opportunities to address gathered crowds, whilst others are gifted in making the most of the opportunities within daily life. Whatever the context or opportunity, Advance is committed to keeping proclamation at the heart of evangelism, that those we encounter would hear the gospel explained in a way they can understand, and be given an opportunity to accept its truth.

Advance groups mentor people such as Mo, who having moved from a life of crime by the power of the gospel whilst serving time in prison, now leads a thriving church ministry in Hull which reaches out powerfully to those on the margins of society, and is seeing people come to faith week-in-week-out, 'My Advance group experience helps me keep the gospel at the centre of everything we do in and through the church, and I'm constantly encouraged, inspired and challenged by the guys in the group to keep stepping out.'

Then there is Amanda who came to faith through a local church running an Alpha course, the leader of which also runs an Advance group. Amanda joined Advance and began to learn about how to not only live in the new faith she had, but to step out and speak out even as a brand new Christian, "I was excited about my new faith in Jesus, but was amazed to find out he wants to use me to help others discover his love even while I'm still learning about him and growing in my own faith.'

Benny is a teenager who began to feel a specific call upon his life to preach the gospel from platforms and stages. Through

Advance, Benny developed his preaching gift and a deeper understanding of the gospel before stepping out to preach to more than 1,000 of his peers at an evangelistic youth concert where many hundreds gave their lives to Jesus. 'It was nerve-racking for me to speak in front of so many people, but I knew that God was calling and empowering me to do it, and that Advance had helped me prepare for the responsibility,' he says.

Lauren recently stepped out to pray for and lead her Muslim taxi driver to Jesus as she explained who He truly is to the driver over the course of a single journey, and was able to connect him to a local church. She said, 'I always want to share my faith with anyone I meet, and Advance has helped me to be bold and clear in every opportunity, even when it's a bit scary!'

These are just some of the stories of those in the Advance movement who are stepping out to share the gospel. Advance groups exist for any who take the gospel call seriously, so they can be equipped, empowered and encouraged as they go, that we would partner with the King in the advancement of His Kingdom until He returns.

Yes, but How?

For you:

1 To whom and where does God want you to reach out with his love?
2 Are you praying for opportunities to share the gospel?
3 What do you find most challenging about this?

For your group:

1 Are you praying daily for individuals by name to come to know Jesus? Can you as a group pray for some of one another's people as well? Why not petition as a group for people to meet Jesus?
2 Have you seen wonders accompany your words and works?
3 Why not pray for boldness right now together?

Resources

'Great Commission' exists to equip you to confidently share your faith, fuelling a passion to make Jesus known. It's an online evangelism hub—greatcommission.co.uk—that connects you to a wide range of stories, tools, and initiatives for sharing Jesus.

As people whose lives have been changed by Jesus, we all have a story to share. But sometimes we can struggle to find the words to talk about what Jesus has done. That's why this evangelism hub wants to not only inspire a passion for sharing Jesus, but also empower us to have the confidence to talk about him.

The site celebrates the fact that people are coming to faith across the UK by sharing inspiring stories of lives transformed by Jesus. It collaborates with hundreds of organizations by signposting to a wide range of evangelistic initiatives, tools, and stories. The site encourages us all to pray more for those who don't yet know Jesus, so that the Holy Spirit would give us the confidence to share Jesus wherever we are. Check it out at www.greatcommission.co.uk.

Some great evangelistic courses:

www.alpha.org

www.christianityexplored.org

The Natural Evangelism Course (available from www.canonjjohn
.com/store/books)

Further Reading:

P. Knox, *Story Bearer* (London: IVP, 2020)

G. Calver, A. Calver, *Gamechangers* (Oxford: Monarch Books, 2016)

9

Signs of the Times

'In our rushing, bulls in china shops, we break our own lives.'

Ann Voskamp

The Acts church had their own unique culture that affected how people were living and how they received Jesus. It's important for us to consider how different our own culture looks today and what that means for sharing Jesus in words, works, and wonders. We are living in an extraordinary time. Life is moving so fast, everything feels like it is changing before our eyes, and technology has never developed this quickly. We continue to live in what many have dubbed the 'digital revolution' or as the 'third industrial revolution'. It has not finished yet, but is exhausting to live in the middle of. The American church pastor John Mark Comer writes extensively about hurrying in his latest book: 'I live in one of the most secular, post-Christian cities in our nation (Portland, USA), and the longer I'm here, the more convinced I become that hurry is the issue under all the other issues. [It's] The root cause beneath so much of the anger and anxiety of our cultural moment. And followers of Jesus are not immune to culture's pain.'[1] We certainly are rushing around, and it is having an impact on us all.

The pace of life is making so much of what needs to be treasured instead appear instant, is putting a strain on people to deliver quickly, and is changing the way we as individuals, and as a society, are wired and shaped. The Christian futurologist Patrick Dixon puts it this way: 'The developed world is cash-rich, time-poor and feels intensely impatient. Chapters of personal lives are measured in minutes, major events in seconds. Five billion people are communicating digitally, usually many times an hour on mobiles, unless asleep. There is a widespread obsession with instant information, answers, new products and new friends.'[2] This has all had a massive impact on our attention spans as a result of the world we are part of. The ability to focus on a specific task is vital in life and yet attention spans have been decreasing over the last twenty years with the massive increase in external communication. In the year 2000 the average attention span was 12 seconds. In 2015 this had gone down to 8.25 seconds, which is less than a goldfish which has an attention span of 9 seconds.[3] All this has an impact on our ability to focus fully on time with God. Moreover, it's very discouraging to the preachers amongst us that we will have the attention of some of those listening for 8.25 seconds!

So much of this rapid change has been fuelled by the addition of an extra limb to so many—their phone. It's not even a generational thing. When either of our sets of parents come to visit, they are as glued to a screen as any other age group. When we think of our kids growing up as digital natives, it will be fascinating to see how they work through technology with any children they may later have. An article in the *New York Times* talked about the use of our phones saying, 'Smartphones are our constant companions. For many of us, their glowing screens are a ubiquitous presence, drawing us in with endless diversions, like the warm ping of social approval delivered in the forms of likes and retweets, and the algorithmically amplified outrage of the latest "breaking" news or controversy. They're in our hands, as soon as we wake, and command our attention until the final moments before we fall asleep. Steve Jobs would not approve.'[4] This was never what they were supposed to be. John Mark Comer says that 'the iPhone is a greater threat to western Christianity than secularism ever will be.'[5] He argues that the distraction it is causing is the greatest threat to our walk with the Lord. It's also fascinating that Apple has introduced a screen time monitoring app just as many of their executives have kids starting to use their products. They know how potentially negative the effect of their own devices can be on their own offspring.

The internet, too, has changed so much. It's founder, Tim Berners-Lee, feels very mixed in his assessment of how this tool has been used. On the one hand, what a gift to the world, and on the other, he is 'devastated' at how it has been misused and is causing many problems.[6] Indeed, many tech insiders working in Silicon Valley have expressed grave concern at how their inventions can go on to have such a devastating impact on so many, to the point of even being compared to drug use.[7] It's fascinating that so many of these tech experts are restricting, or banning altogether, the use of the products they helped create by their own children.

As well as just being busy and in a rush, there are many who are spending all their time pursuing stuff they aren't even passionate about. Former England cricketer Andrew Flintoff writes 'So many people spend a large chuck of their lives doing something they don't enjoy. They're no different from bees, or those ants you see carrying leaves on their backs, it's just in a bigger scale. They're all just working to keep things working, but to what end?'[8] For so much of life today, it feels like many are stuck on a treadmill of survival in the face of a rapidly changing landscape.

Yet we Christians have another way. We need to put the phone down, turn the iPad off, and realize that we have direct access to something far more powerful, beneficial, and life changing. We need to stop desperately waiting for our latest dopamine hit from a Facebook 'like' or Twitter retweet and instead focus on something far more essential. We need to know the power our devices have over us and be released from this to focus on something far greater. After all, there's a reason that 'researchers liken our smartphones to slot machines, triggering the same reward pathways in our brain.'[9] The American church leader Tim Keller says that 'the only person who dares wake up a king at 3 a.m. for a glass of water is a child. We have that kind of access.' We have direct access to the Saviour of the World and must not lose touch with him due to the madness of the rest of life.

A Secular Age?

We are living in an incredibly secular time. Many want faith wiped off the cultural landscape. In his book, *How (Not) to be Secular*, James K. A. Smith challenges Charles Taylor's monumental work, *A Secular Age*. Smith makes a courageous attempt to show that it's possible to live differently than the prevailing norm. He is honest about how complex faith can be and shows great concern and compassion for those caught up in the realities of our secular age. He also makes it clear that it's incredibly difficult to ever accept that there is definitely nothing out there. He puts it this way: 'The doubter's doubt is faith; his temptation is belief, and it is a temptation that has not been entirely quelled, even in a secular age'[10]

For many, they still hope that there might be more than this. That humanity and all it's problems needn't be the ultimate entity in the cosmos. The writer Julian Barnes famously said, when asked if he believes in anything greater, that 'I don't believe in God, but I miss Him.'[11] For so many, there is a desire for an almighty and a hope for more. In science they famously say that 'there is always a trace.' With people, it feels much the same. The Lord made everyone, and as such, has left a trace or a fingerprint on everyone. Ecclesiastes 3:11 puts it this way: 'He has made everything beautiful in its time. He has also set eternity in the human heart; yet no one can fathom what God has done from beginning to end.' However secular the culture, there is still a trace in every heart.

Additionally, at some point every culture makes some kind of puritanical shift back. After all, the church in Corinth is not more morally bankrupt today than it was when Paul wrote to it. As a society becomes ever more morally bankrupt, there will at some point be a secular overstep that will lead to a more conservative world-view. Many would argue that in the UK some of this has already started. An example of this would be that the proportion of sixteen-to twenty-four-year-olds who do not drink alcohol increased from 18% in 2005 to 29% in 2015.[12] We grew up as part of 'generation binge' in the days of Brit-pop and 'Cool Britannia'—a season in the 1990s when we all felt like a member of the rock 'n' roll generation, and the UK delighted as British music became the 'in' thing all over the planet.[13] Today's young people appear to be quite a contrast to those days. In his book, *Disappearing Church*, Mark Sayers talks of this generation of young people as wanting the kingdom but not the King. Issues like justice, peace, and equality define what younger people want in a western world. These are values of the kingdom and are wanted by those younger. They just don't seem to want the King too.[14] He notes elsewhere that the secularists' myth is the idea of progress without presence; it is simply not possible.[15] In time we hope and pray that the desire for the King will match that for the values of the kingdom, and that real progress will be made alongside the presence of the living God, but in the short-term, it seems that perhaps the puritanical shift has already begun?

Junction Moments

Prior to serving at the Evangelical Alliance, I, Gavin, spent fourteen years working for Youth for Christ. We loved seeing many young people come to faith and were constantly encouraged by quite how many did so. It remains a great highlight to ever meet an adult who came to faith as a teenager through YFC. We were quite taken with Wes Stafford's (from Compassion USA) image that when it comes to evangelism, young people are like 'wet cement' and older people are 'dry cement.' In other words, it's a lot easier to make a profound impact on a young life. Therefore, as a church we must keep pouring value and resource into youth and children's ministry. As our friend the chairman of Care for the Family, Rob Parsons, says, 'If your church roof has a hole in it, stick a bucket under it but don't stop pouring resources into youth and children's ministry.'

Since joining EA it's become more important to find out when older people might be more likely to come to faith. Yes, the greatest fruitfulness in our witnessing may well continue to be amongst younger generations, but we do need to be aware of what might be significant in older generations too. Most adults seem to come to faith at 'junction moments.' Such occasions are when there is a drastic life change (for better or worse) that brings us out of the normal everyday realities of life. For example, you get married, lose your job, move to a different area, lose a loved one, have a baby, etc. Such moments make us question life a lot more and look for answers to the deeper things. Therefore, as a starting point, we the church need to be there for people as they face these moments. Let's not be so busy with our own lives and church programmes that we miss these times for others.

I, Gavin, was out running a while ago, and I had an overwhelming sense that the Lord was pointing out that the whole of the UK will be facing a 'junction moment' of it's own over the next few years. Whatever we think about the current political landscape, however we voted over Brexit, and whatever our assessment is of the UK's spiritual health there's little doubt that much uncertainty lies ahead. No one fully knows what this season holds for this nation, and many of the things people thought they could rely on seem in doubt. Within all this change, and possible chaos, the openness to the gospel is potentially far greater than when things are much calmer and straightforward.

This current 'junction moment' provides us, the church, with a wonderful opportunity to show what is different when we, too, face this uncertainty, but we do so with Jesus. How does this impact the way we behave? What difference should it make to our sense of hopefulness? How can we help others who don't know Jesus to see in us the difference this makes? Way back to the start of the Bible in Genesis 1 is the reality that the only thing that truly brings order out of chaos is the Lord. Therefore, let's pray he does the same in our land at this time.

We find ourselves in a season when much is up in the air and the certainty we have in Jesus is seemingly even more counter-cultural than ever. The Archbishop of Canterbury, Justin Welby, writes that 'moments of change are moments of great hope and opportunity. They are usually surrounded by threats, perceived or real, but the opportunity to spring-clean the detritus of culture and habit at a national level is a gift and not a danger.'[16] This is a moment of profound change, and we the church need to take this opportunity to impact our land profoundly.

Mark Sayers goes a step further still by encouraging us that in this time of tumultuous culture change, we need to reframe this entire cultural moment from a profound crisis into a wonderful opportunity.[17] Now is a moment to let your salt bring flavour and your light shine even more than normal. It's a chance for our faith in Jesus to lead us to even greater holiness and distinctiveness, and out of this, for many to come to know him too. We certainly don't have all the answers and may also be concerned about the future. However, in contrast to the world, we can hold to that often quoted saying 'I don't know what the future holds, but I know who holds the future.' We can live in the assurance of the presence and plans of God at a time when the nation is struggling.

Let's not miss the opportunity presented to us to see many of those we know impacted for the gospel as we all face this 'junction moment' together. Let's turn this cultural crisis into an opportunity.

Attacked for Speaking Out

As ever, with great opportunity, also comes strong opposition. We seem to be living in a time when the world is trying to gag Christians from having any views outside of perceived cultural orthodoxy. There is a growing temptation to baptize our culture when in fact what is needed is something different in a morally disintegrating nation. Anyone who dares to speak up or stand out is quickly attacked by a culture claiming to do so as an act of tolerance.

The preacher Jeff Lucas put it this way in a magazine column 'Some of those who want to lead us over the cliff often insist that they are the only ones who are right and we disagree with the crowd at our peril. Liberal fundamentalism rules. If I disagree with the popular consensus, then I'm quickly tagged as hateful or bigoted, one who must be silenced or banished immediately. It's ironic, because if we differ in our convictions and opinions, we're accused of being intolerant—and that won't be tolerated.'[18]

It would be so easy to just step back and not bother, but what do we have left if the people of God are bullied out of their beliefs? Where in the history of the church has the culture it finds itself in mirrored what it stands for? We need to be distinct. The opportunities for our message of hope in a culture of despair has never been so great and yet the temptation to keep quiet is almost intoxicating. Nowhere does this feel more true than in social media. We used to love using it, but these days it can often feel like a war zone.

I, Gavin, in particular, am often attacked on Twitter. At the time it feels like the end of the world, but in truth, we need to step away and know what the Lord thinks of us even though some of the interaction feels like a digital equivalent of the early Christians being thrown to the lions. The illiberal and intolerant liberal voices can be so oppressive and yet this must not stop us. The worst of all is when it's 'friendly fire' from other Christians. Some of this is impossible to explain rationally and away from a short character limit. This was highlighted best by a tweet I received that read '@GavCalver you are the scum of the earth and will burn in hell for a long time #lovewins.'

The challenges, though, must not make us downhearted, and we must avoid feeling too sorry for ourselves. Tim Keller says that 'rather than thinking of ourselves as an embattled political minority or persecuted underdogs, Christians should be overflowing with the joy of our salvation that we feel the privilege of singing his praises to those who do not know him.'[19] The joy of knowing Jesus should stop us naval-gazing and instead help us to realize that we have the most wonderful gift to offer the world.

We also need to know what our freedoms are to share the gospel. If we listened to some parts of the media, we'd think that we weren't allowed to ever share our faith or pray for others. But the law doesn't say this. In the UK we have almost more gospel freedom than anywhere else in the world. However, we must use these freedoms or our children, and children's children, will lose them. In his work at the EA, Gavin has been involved in a project called Speak Up. This is a project works alongside the Lawyers Christian Fellowship that provides Christians with a simple and clear understanding of our gospel freedoms. EA thought this wouldn't be that well used, but over 100,000 people have already accessed it. We need to know our actual freedoms before moaning about those we perceive we are losing.

We must speak up, live out, and share our faith in our cultural landscape, however challenging. Francis Chan says that 'part of your responsibility in the Body of Christ is to help set the pace for the Church by listening and obeying and living Christ. Knowing that God has called us each to live faithful and devoted lives before Him, by the power of His Spirit.'[20] We may not always go as far and as fast as everyone else, but we can set a pace for others to follow that relentlessly pursues Jesus regardless of the landscape we find ourselves living in.

Yes, but How?

For you:

Listen:

There are many ways of reading the signs of the times, but we highly recommend listening to the 'This Cultural Moment' podcast. Each episode is about following Jesus in the post-Christian world. It explores the secular, progressive, post-Christian world in which we live and asks how followers of Jesus are meant to engage. It is a collaboration between John Mark Comer of Bridgetown Church in Portland, USA, and Mark Sayers of Red Church in Melbourne, Australia. **https://thisculturalmoment.com**

For your group:

Speak Up:

Speak Up is designed to equip and inspire Christians with confidence and knowledge of the current legal freedoms we have to share our faith.

The good news of Jesus is something we all have a part in sharing. Through our everyday lives—at the local playground, at the bus stop, or over a cup of tea—we all have amazing opportunities to introduce people to Jesus.

We won't always be sure how it will be received, but the Christian message must be proclaimed. Romans 10:14 says "And how can they believe in the one of whom they have not heard? And how can they hear without someone preaching to them?" In this country we've got the freedom and privilege of being able to speak up and demonstrate the love of God and the transforming power of Jesus in our communities.

Why not get hold of Speak Up and chat together about it? Get a copy of it here: https://www.eauk.org/what-we-do/initiatives/speak-up.

For Parents:

Care for the Family's Katherine Hill has written a great book entitled *Left to their own devices?* It will help parents to be confident in raising their kids in a world full of screens.

Further Reading:

J. M. Comer, *The Ruthless Elimination of Hurry* (Colorado Springs: Waterbrook Press, 2019)

M. Sayers, *Reappearing Church* (Chicago: Moody Press, 2019)

10

The Gospel

'There is a power in God's gospel beyond all description.'

Charles Spurgeon

I, Anne, recall jogging in France a number of years ago, and on my route I would always pass by a beautiful old church. If I happened to be out there on a Sunday morning, the bells would chime and it would make me smile. One time when I ran past it, I felt a strange heaviness of heart. Yes, it looked stunning on the outside, the grounds around it were immaculate, and it had such central prominence in the pretty little village, but something was bothering me. I just had a sense in my guts of the Lord saying, 'Anne, it may look lovely on the outside, but it is what is on the inside that matters.' A short time ago I was reminded of the Disney classic *Sleeping Beauty*. Our daughter, Amelie, is a teenager so I was not recalling it because we had just watched it. Across my mind's eye I kept seeing Sleeping Beauty asleep in the huge four poster bed, holding the single rose on her chest, behind the thick stone castle walls. Then I would see the dense, intense forest that had built up over 100 years. Into the forest I could see the prince coming, riding with his sword, cutting through the thick undergrowth, slaying the fire-breathing dragon, and fighting his way all the way to Sleeping Beauty. Now, you all know what he does next? That's right, he bends down and kisses her awake, and what does the kiss symbolize? Yes, true love's kiss—not just any old kiss, but the kiss of genuine love, and she awakens.

My sense was that the Lord was saying, firstly that, he was coming to awaken his bride, his church, with true love, with the kiss of resurrection power. Suddenly I was seeing the Prince of Peace riding through the forest, slaying the enemy, beating his way all the way to his children, to us, because he loves us so, so much. Secondly, I knew that the Lord, and he alone, had the power to come swiftly through the debris in our lives, to cut through the debris, and he was on a urgent mission to wake up his church. There is no time to lose! Thirdly, I also felt Jesus was turning my attention to the prince, and I saw him in the depths of the forest, in the darkness, in the intensity of the thorns and brambles, struggling to see his way through. The prince became like us. My sense was that the Lord was showing me that many of his children feel totally surrounded by darkness, in pain, with heavy oppression on them, and they cannot see a way through. The Lord was putting the sword of the Spirit into the prince's hand and effectively saying 'Use this. You can get through with this.' Scripture says that 'the sword of the Spirit is the Word of God' (Ephesians 6:17). The power of the Word of God, feasting on his Word and allowing the Holy Spirit to minister through it, will lead to awesome breakthroughs. All of that from *Sleeping Beauty*— not bad, hey?

We do not know what happens in that lovely old church in France, but we do know that the Lord of all is coming to breathe life into his people, to pour his love into our hearts, and make us a dangerous people like those we witness in Acts.

Throughout Acts, we see the Spirit moving very differently at each turn. Yes, there is a sense of journey with the early followers travelling from place to place to minister, but there is also a sense of movement as the apostles do not continue to look the same, or act the same, or just go through the regular motions. The Spirit brings life to them that keeps them on the move in ways they would not imagine or expect.

We hear Jesus commission his followers to 'go and make disciples of all nations, baptizing them in the name of the Father and of the Son and of the Holy Spirit, and teaching them to obey everything I have commanded you. And surely I am with you always, to the very end of the age' (Matthew 28:19-20). The word 'go' is active. He does not say 'sit' and let me make disciples, he tells all of them to go. Then as we move into Acts, we can see the empowering of the Holy Spirit in the outworking of the Commission. The old churches are beautiful, but are we using them to fulfill, the call of Christ? Are they full of his life? We are deeply challenged.

When we begin to ask 'How Lord? How do we fulfil this mandate? What does it look like?' We are struck by the constant reality of words, works, and wonders in making disciples. It is not one without the other, but all three, along with all the gifts we have, working together. The apostles performed many miraculous signs and wonders among the people (Acts 5:12) – wonders. The believers keep meeting together and people bring their sick to them (Acts 5:12,15) = works and wonders. The apostles break free from prison and teach in the temple courts (Acts 5:25) = wonders and words. When we move into Acts 6, we see works going on to look after the widows, and we also hear Stephen's words being preached, as well as wonders worked out through him (6:1,8; 7:2). There is not really one without the others because the Holy Spirit is always at work to minister through the words and actions of the saints.

In Romans, Paul says, 'I will not venture to speak of anything except what Christ has accomplished through me in leading the Gentiles to obey God by what I have said and done—by the power of signs and miracles, through the power of the Holy Spirit. So from Jerusalem all the way around to Illyricum, I have fully proclaimed the gospel of Christ' (Romans 15:18-19). For Paul, proclaiming the 'full' gospel involves what he says, does, and the power of signs and miracles. If we are going to fully work out the Great Commission in our landscape, we desperately need to see an increase of the power of the Holy Spirit. We long not just to be preaching, teaching, and doing nice things for people, but for signs and wonders to play an increased part in these endeavours.

At the back of our 'Encounter' venue at Spring Harvest, a woman was painting during the Bible teaching. She drew a gigantic wave, telling me, Anne, that the paper wasn't big enough for the wave that the Lord was showing her. Next to the wave she wrote some very challenging words: 'Big swell coming. Train hard.' Prepare well. Get ready to catch it! Ride it well.' As I read these words and looked at the picture, I felt a ripple of pins and needles (the Holy Spirit) through my body, and my immediate thought was 'I cannot ride that wave. I am no good at surfing!'

As we pray and pen this book, we do sense a wave coming and we wonder if we are not already in the shallows of what is to come. If that is indeed the case, then how are we going to get ready to ride the wave? We can only hope to ride it with the power of the Holy Spirit, if we are trained by him to minister in words, works, and wonders. If we are not interested then the wave will pass us by, but for those of us who have a hunger and a passion to be part of what the Lord is going to do through his church, we best get ready.

The disciples had to go to Jerusalem and wait. And pray. Then empowered by the Holy Spirit, they didn't give up praying but they began to ride the greatest wave in history so far.

But there will be another one, and the best way we can learn how to ride is to read, remember, pray, and wait, asking for the holy equipping of the Most-High God. As the Spirit begins to increase his power and momentum throughout the nations, so the enemy will rise from his slumber and do all he can to halt the advance of the kingdom.

We are always relieved to think that God works with all of us, no matter what, to spread his Word. However, what could we do differently so that our words carry greater authority, our wonders are purely from the throne room, and our works are selflessly driven? 'The early church didn't need the energetic music, great videos, attractive leaders, or elaborate lighting to be excited about being part of God's body. The pure gospel was enough to put them in a place of awe.'[1] We are working very hard to be attractive to the lost and the broken, but by what means? It is so challenging to think that if the fullness of the gospel were really alive with the power of the Holy Spirit, how much would we look to worldly resources? I, Anne, was so aware on my return from ministering amongst the Iranian church that I could not mention it on social media. What had happened was so incredible and looked so like the early church, I wanted to shout about it. However, so much of what is going on is happening underground to protect the believers. Isn't it ironic that the works of God that are the most awesome are often happening in the hidden places? Have we somehow put our confidence in people, in stages, in lights, and in bands to the point where we are leaving out the most vital ingredient: the Lord himself? Perhaps we would see more wonders accompanying our words and works if we just got out of the way and let God be God.

There is a trumpet call sounding over the church calling the people of God to turn and listen and look at him—to once again surrender, to once again admit that we do not have the answers and we do not know the way, and that we long for the Lord himself to lead us. We do not want to continue in old patterns because we are comfortable in them. Equally, we do not want to do something new that comes from our own human desires. Alan Scott says 'The great need of our day is scattered servants, kingdom carriers who have learnt to move beyond phenomena in services to release power in their everyday lives.'[2] Our heart's cry is to see a supernatural equipping breathe life into the saints and set our pulses racing with hunger and passion to see a nation changed. We can carry on preaching and attending services, but encountering the Living Lord and asking him to move is what will transform the world.

The believers pray: 'Now Lord consider their threats and enable your servants to speak your word with great boldness. Stretch out your hand to heal and perform miraculous signs and wonders through the name of your holy servant, Jesus. After they prayed, the place where they were meeting was shaken. And they were all filled with the Holy Spirit and spoke the word of God boldly (Acts 4:29-31).'

Opposition

We cannot talk about the power of the Holy Spirit coming, the miraculous signs and wonders, the spread of the gospel, the unity amongst the believers, and the lives continuing to be transformed without also noticing the challenging backdrop. We would rather talk about these great bits in Acts and just encourage the church to go for it in the power of the Holy Spirit—after all, we are both 'cup-half-full' kind of people. However, that would not do justice to the text or the reality for Christians around the world. If we are to truly engage in words, works, and wonders, there will be opposition, there will be persecution, and there will be disagreement. We see all these things peppered throughout the narrative. As the Lord advances through his people in power, there are many who try to stop it. Look at Stephen being stoned to death (Acts 7:54-60), James being killed (Acts 12:2), great persecution (Acts 8:1), imprisonment (Acts 12,16), and disagreement (15:39-40). The enemy is at work to try and halt the mission of God.

One of the ways we need to train to ride the wave and advance in the power of the Spirit is to learn how to arm ourselves for battle. Sometimes we are aware that we go through life asking God to move mightily and are stepping into opportunities that we pray will advance the gospel, and then something will go wrong at home, or we will argue with someone, or fear and nightmares begin to fill our minds. Then we step back and think, 'Oh yes, we might get some attack. Now what do we do?'

Bad things do happen but what we notice with the believers in Acts is that they never stop praying: they press in with prayer when Peter is in jail (Acts 12:5), they appoint the Seven to oversee the ministry to the widows so that they can keep praying (Acts 6:4), they join together constantly in prayer (Acts 1:14). They are always laying hands and praying, covering everything in prayer. We are so challenged that the ministry we do has to be saturated in prayer. It doesn't mean bad things won't happen. We see that they still happen throughout Acts. It doesn't mean we are always safe, but it does mean we are equipped and ready for the attack, and aware that God is with us.

Paul encourages us to 'put on the full armour of God to take our stand against the devil's schemes' (Ephesians 6:10-17) and to 'pray in the Spirit on all occasions with all kinds of prayers and requests' (6:18). We put great value on doing, on serving, on working, on relaxing, but do we put value on prayer and meeting with the Lord? On arming ourselves properly for the battles that might come?

If we really mean business about seeing wonders added to our words and works, if we are really desperate to press in with prayer and hungry to see a move of God, if we have a vision of seeing God's kingdom come here on earth and we are beginning to do something about it, then we automatically position ourselves on the front line, facing enemy attack. Thankfully, as we have already seen, this is not uncommon in Scripture. Just before great breakthrough comes great warfare, we just need to be well armed to deal with it.

Nehemiah's Blueprint

Nehemiah gives us an incredible framework for dealing with opposition. There he is seeking to rebuild the wall around Jerusalem, having had his heart broken over the Jews in exile and longing for them to return to their city, he faces attack on every side. Let's look at chapter 6 as a tool for enabling us to tackle what might well come against us as we build the church.

Firstly, as he begins to build there is repeated distraction: 'Sanballat and Geshem sent me this message: 'Come let us meet together in one of the villages on the plain of Ono … four times they sent me the same message, and each time I gave them the same answer' (6:2,4). The enemy is not creative, but you can guarantee that he is consistent. He plays the same record over and over, and we can find ourselves stuck with the same narrative in our minds. The enemy wants to lead us back into slavery, away from freedom, and so he will keep on distracting you in whatever way seems to work.

Nehemiah's enemies try to distract him, and they also try to make accusations. Sanballat sends an accusing letter: 'It is reported among the nations—and Geshem says it is true—that you and the Jews are plotting to revolt and therefore you are building the wall. Moreover, you are about to become their King and even appointed prophets' (6:6-7). Right into Nehemiah's hands falls a lie that says, 'Not only do I think this, but others think this is true too.' The liar comes right to him announcing 'You might think you are doing this with the right motive, but we know what the real truth is.' The deceiver approaches us with accusations. There may well be people who misread our motives and distort what is truth. We need to know who we are as sons and daughters of the King and have deep clarity over what we know we are called to do.

Thirdly, accusations are also lies. Nehemiah replies to Sanballat: 'I sent him this reply—nothing like what you are saying is happening; you are just making it up out of your head' (6:8). Lies are a key tactic of the enemy. He wants to stop us in our tracks and will fill our minds with lies about who we are and what we are doing. The Lord wants us to declare truth, not to mull over the lies and let them take root, but go deep into the Word of God and proclaim it over ourselves.

Fourthly, we encounter fear: Nehemiah's enemies try and sow fear into him by saying 'This report will get back to the King' (6:7)—we will tell him what you are really trying to do.' In verse 9, Nehemiah recognizes the strategy: 'They were all trying to frighten us.' Fear is what keeps us from advancing in faith. Fear cripples us, keeps us where we are, and stops us from moving into all God has for us. Nehemiah realizes that his enemies had been hired to intimidate him (6:13), so that he would be so frightened and overawed that he couldn't complete the call on his life.

Fifthly, weakness is used as a tactic to try and make the people give up, but Nehemiah recognizes it in verse 9: 'Their hands will get too weak.' The enemy likes to continually remind us that we are too weak to do what God has called us to do. He tells us that we are not up to it, we cannot complete the work; it's impossible, forget it. Nehemiah realizes that the deceiver is at work: 'I realized that God had not sent him, but that he had prophesied against me because Tobiah and Sanballat had hired him' (6:12). Things may appear good and right, but it is not the narrow path to life, it is the broad road to destruction. The enemy will beckon us 'come this way it will be easier,' but no, it is not the route to life with Jesus.

Finally we witness Nehemiah's realizing that his enemy was trying to draw him into sin: 'He had been hired to intimidate me so that I might commit a sin by doing this and then they would give me a bad name to discredit me' (6:13). All the time, the enemy is intent on leading us into sin. He wants us to sin against God, hurt God, and distance us from him.

The reason we point to this passage is that Nehemiah shows us a way out of the mess, a way of taking on the deceiver so that he can continue to advance with the mission of God. He does not get sucked in but finds a way of combatting the attack. He *realized* what was happening: 'They were scheming to harm me' (6:2). He recognizes the oppressor at work. Lord, give us this kind of discernment! Then he *names* the attack: 'They were trying to frighten us, thinking, their hands will get too weak for the work and it will not be completed' (6:9). Nehemiah *sees* what is going on and believes God over man. Lord, please speak more loudly than any other voice!

Nehemiah does not get *distracted*: 'I am carrying on a great project and cannot go down' (6:3); he stays focussed on the end goal. We need to keep going and finish well. It is a marathon, not a sprint. Keep our eyes on Jesus, not on the problem. Nehemiah does not get drawn off on a tangent. Then Nehemiah *addresses it* head-on because it comes again and again: 'Nothing like what you are saying is happening, you are just making it up' (6:8). He does not ignore what is happening but he deals with it swiftly. The lies don't consume his time and attention. He *declares* the truth rather than letting the lie invade and take root in his mind.

Absolutely, crucially, Nehemiah prays, 'Now strengthen my hands' (6:9)—the perfect counter attack. Effectively, he says, 'That's a lie, and this is the truth.' When you feel low, praise him; when you feel ungrateful, thank him; when you sense the darkness in your heart and mind, worship him.

What amazes us in the text is that Nehemiah stands strong and keeps building. He says, 'Should a man like me run away?' (6:11). He does not quit. Sometimes we just need to stand still and let the Lord fight for us. As Pharoah and the Egyptians approach the Israelites before they cross the Red Sea, they are terrified, but Moses says, 'Do not be afraid. Stand firm and you will see the deliverance the Lord will bring you today. The Egyptians you see today you will never see again. The Lord will fight for you; you need only to be still' (Exodus 14:13-14). Whatever you are facing, do not be pulled to the left or the right, stay focussed on where you are and what God is calling you to. Nehemiah is such an example to us of someone who persevered through the fight and completed the commission on his life. The wall was completed in fifty-two days! (6:15).

Our sister Vicky always ends her letters or emails with 'Keep going'—such an encouragement whatever we are facing. We can all learn from this. Even when things are really tough, let's keep moving forward in the face of the storm.

If we really want to see the church unleashed into every area of society, and to build the church even when the gates of hell try to rage against it, then know this: there is a real enemy at large. He is defeated, but he will not be thrown down until the King of Kings returns for his bride. The more that we can equip ourselves to fight, the more we will advance and see his kingdom come on earth as it is in heaven.

Yes, but How?

For you:

1 Do you feel awake?
2 What opposition are you facing?
3 Take some time to ask the Lord to help you face the giants around you and to be fully alive in him.

For your group:

1 Do you sense a wake-up call being sounded over the church? Or have you heard others talking about this? What do you think?
2 How do you sense God might be 'waking up' his people?
3 Why not work your way down the opposition list from Nehemiah (outlined in this chapter). Which one/s do you relate to and why? Pray together.

A couple of ideas other churches have implemented for reaching out...

1 Lark in the park

Lark in the Park is a community event run by local churches in Sidcup, Thanet, and Woking during the summer. It is an amazing local event that draws the churches together to serve, reach, and bless their community locally. Something of this scale may be too much for you to try, but how about a community fun day, or the like, to impact locally. For more information on Lark in the Park, do visit www .larkinthepark.com.

2 #doyouknowHim?

The idea of #doyouknowHim? came about when the team at one of the churches in Skipton was planning for an Easter outreach. The question seemed to lend itself not only to those who already know Jesus but are challenged to know him more, but also to anyone who has never thought about the fact that Jesus knows and loves them, and desperately wants us to know and love him. It asks 'Have you met Jesus? Do you know Him? And if you do know him, how well do you know Jesus?' Like any relationship, there is always the need to invest time, effort, and heart to make it grow. This initiative has been great at strengthening the church and reaching the community. Find out more at www.doyouknowhim.net.

Further Reading:

R.T. Kendall, *Prepare your Heart for the Midnight Cry* (London: SPCK, 2016)
A. Hirsch, M.Nelson, *Reframation* (100 Movements, 2019)

Part 4

UNLEASHED
POTENTIAL

Acts 8:4–8 and 26–40

Acts 8:4-8, 26-40

Philip in Samaria

Those who had been scattered preached the word wherever they went. ⁵Philip went down to a city in Samaria and proclaimed the Messiah there. ⁶When the crowds heard Philip and saw the signs he performed, they all paid close attention to what he said. ⁷For with shrieks, impure spirits came out of many, and many who were paralyzed or lame were healed. ⁸So there was great joy in that city.

Philip and the Ethiopian

Now an angel of the Lord said to Philip, 'Go south to the road—the desert road—that goes down from Jerusalem to Gaza.' ²⁷So he started out, and on his way he met an Ethiopian eunuch, an important official in charge of all the treasury of the Kandake (which means 'queen of the Ethiopians'). This man had gone to Jerusalem to worship, ²⁸and on his way home was sitting in his chariot reading the Book of Isaiah the prophet. ²⁹The Spirit told Philip, 'Go to that chariot and stay near it.'

³⁰Then Philip ran up to the chariot and heard the man reading Isaiah the prophet. 'Do you understand what you are reading?' Philip asked.

³¹'How can I,' he said, 'unless someone explains it to me?' So he invited Philip to come up and sit with him.

³² This is the passage of Scripture the eunuch was reading:

> He was led like a sheep to the slaughter,
>   and as a lamb before its shearer is silent,
>   so he did not open his mouth.
> ³³ In his humiliation he was deprived of justice.
>   Who can speak of his descendants?
>   For his life was taken from the earth.

³⁴ The eunuch asked Philip, 'Tell me, please, who is the prophet talking about, himself or someone else?' ³⁵ Then Philip began with that very passage of Scripture and told him the good news about Jesus.

³⁶ As they traveled along the road, they came to some water and the eunuch said, 'Look, here is water. What can stand in the way of my being baptized?' ³⁸ And he gave orders to stop the chariot. Then both Philip and the eunuch went down into the water and Philip baptized him. ³⁹ When they came up out of the water, the Spirit of the Lord suddenly took Philip away, and the eunuch did not see him again, but went on his way rejoicing. ⁴⁰ Philip, however, appeared at Azotus and traveled about, preaching the gospel in all the towns until he reached Caesarea.

11

Encounter in the Desert

'Have the ability to look in another direction. A small shift could guide you to the real purposes of your life.'

Halle Berry

Spread Out

Stephen has just been stoned to death (Acts 7:54-60), and we have the remarkable moment where Jesus is seen standing at the Father's right-hand side. He would normally be seated, but as the world stones to death a man for his commitment to the Lord, Jesus himself rises to his feet to award Stephen the ultimate standing ovation. This simply made the people persecuting him all the more angry and more determined to end his life as quickly as possible. Saul was delighted and approved of this killing. His anger towards the church was intensifying, and he was determined to utterly destroy the church by whatever means were necessary. This meant that the church had to get mobile, and quickly.

Here at the start of chapter 8 of the book of Acts, we see the church reaching out more widely and getting moving to avoid the intense persecution of its day. Philip has had to leave Jerusalem rapidly following the death of Stephen, but he is certainly not in hiding.[1] He was one of the seven deacons appointed in Acts 6 to make sure the widows were receiving food, but now he is also a preaching evangelist, paving the way for many more to come later, and for those like ourselves today who love to proclaim the gospel.

This wasn't just happening to Philip, though; persecution scattered the church abroad, and everywhere they went they took the gospel with them. They were not running away in fear and hoping not to be caught. No, the early church was determined to be wise but also to spread their message far and wide. Male and Weston put it this way: 'Here is the essential pattern of New Testament evangelism. It was a spontaneous, irrepressible urge to tell other people about the Jesus whom you had met, who had transformed your life.'[2] Once you'd met the risen Jesus you simply could not help but tell others about him. It's that irresistible passion that can't be contained and needs to be set free. In this chapter we see that this freedom then shares all it can wherever the people of God find themselves. Nicky Gumbel says of this chapter that 'nations are comprised of cities, towns and villages. They preached the gospel in all three. Philip preached to a city in Samaria (v.5). Peter and John preached the gospel in many Samaritan villages (v.25). Philip preached the gospel in all the towns until he reached Caesarea (v.40).'[3]

It makes us wonder, how desperate are we to spread the message in the same way? I, Gavin, was at Spring Harvest in 2018 and had an amazing meeting with a passion expert. I'm already fairly naturally passionate, but nonetheless I was keen to hear from her and to learn what makes people passionate and how can you tell what their passions are. She asked me simply, 'Do you know how you can tell what people are most passionate about?' I gave myself a moment to think, then answered, 'I reckon that what they spend their money on is a fairly good clue.' She shut me down and said that my answer could literally not be more wrong. What we spend our money on is entirely socially conditioned, apparently.

I did want the actual answer, though, so I said, 'Okay then, how do you tell?' She said to me there are two simple ways: (1) What people spend their time on. Time is so precious and you only give significant amounts of it to the things you really have to. (2) What people talk about. Apparently, it's impossible to have a half-hour conversation with someone and not hear out of their mouth what they are primarily passionate about. I came away from this encounter so deeply challenged. Am I that passionate about Jesus? Does my time reflect this passion? Can you spend thirty minutes with me in conversation and fail to hear about Jesus? Over the time that's followed, I've often tested in conversation the thirty-minute rule. It has never failed to prove correct that in having a chat of this length with someone, you always hear their primary passions through the natural course of the conversation. I long to be part of a church today in the UK that, like the early church, has that 'spontaneous, irrepressible urge to tell other people about the Jesus we've met, who has transformed our lives.'

The scattering of the Christians at this time led to a huge step forward for the mission of the church. The persecution they were facing in Jerusalem was the catalyst to the spreading of the gospel and the early church. It always seems amazing to us that persecution so often leads to growth of the church. It seems that revivals don't often happen from the church at the mainstream of society but instead when it is at the margins. As the church is pressed, it rises up.

Samaria

As the Christians moved to new areas, they found an incredible openness to the gospel with a huge response to their message. This is shown significantly in Samaria where the people were responding to the gospel Philip preached profoundly, and incredible signs and wonders and a powerful response to the call for baptism accompanied this.[4] There were incredible healings, evil spirits being driven out, and more. The people were captivated by the message they were hearing and were paying really close attention to the message being shared.

We have had the privilege of speaking at all kinds of places, and it strikes us that what was going on in Samaria is well beyond anything we've seen anywhere on the planet. It was like the ultimate Christian outreach mission with so much incredible fruit coming from it. A church under pressure is also an urgent one, and the deep desire for sharing his faith drove Philip to do all he could. This, then coupled with the anointing of the Spirit, led to a time that was simply breathtaking.

It can be so hard to leave what feels like a mountain-top time with the Lord. Most of us will happily walk away from a time in the valley, but when everything seems to be going so well, it feels so natural to stay. We remember this so well from our years serving young people. We ran so many youth residential and festival programmes, and they would be truly amazing. You'd see things that were nothing like normal: there'd often be thousands of teenagers in one place worshipping powerfully, people would get healed, others became Christians, more still felt a call to a ministry or vocation for Jesus. The atmosphere was amazing, the sense of expectation palpable, and the belief that we could change the world for Jesus, tangible.

These times were incredible until it came time to go home. All of a sudden there would be a deep desire from the teenagers to not have to return to their homes and instead to stay with us in the moment. In our minds we had only gathered to then be scattered, but for many young people their confidence in Jesus seemed to wane with every minute closer to going home. When our own youth group would go to such things, they'd return with a desire to be holy and make an impact, but often within weeks, they'd struggle to know what to do, as the feelings seemed to have gone. For many, it seemed more logical to stay in the moment where all the action was happening. We wonder sometimes if that's how it must have felt for Philip in Samaria. Things were going incredibly well, he was being used powerfully, and Jesus felt closer than ever. Why would he ever leave?

Encounter in the Desert

Whatever it was actually like for him in that moment, Philip cannot stay where it is all going so wonderfully. He is given a clear and fresh commission, to go south. We are so challenged by his willingness to do so. He trusts the Lord enough to know that he doesn't know best himself, but God does. We can only ever see part of the picture and not the whole thing whilst the Lord is all-knowing and seeing. Often in our lives we've had to trust God instead of our own desires, and even if it's taken years to see, spiritual hindsight has always shown that the Lord knows best. We so admire Philip for leaving the incredible action and obvious place to minister from a human perspective, and going instead to somewhere seemingly more random and remote. We hope and pray that we would hear the sound of the Lord over the noise of the world and do the same.

When Philip left Samaria, he found himself on the desert road that runs from Jerusalem to Gaza. From a hugely successful ministry situation in the heart of Samaria, he now finds himself in the middle of the desert. Here, in the desert, he meets an Ethiopian eunuch who wanted to have the Scriptures explained to him. So that's what he does. He doesn't preach his pre-prepared talk, he doesn't change the agenda to fit his own intentions, he meets the eunuch where he is. In so much of our outreach to others we need to turn the focus off our agenda and onto what is happening with them. The Lord is always moving, he made everyone, and has left a trace in every human heart; we need to pray for him to lead us in this.

Philip meets the eunuch at his chariot, not in his own comfortable space. We need to be making every effort to engage with those outside of the church where they feel at home and where they will be more open. Let's not let our superficial preferences, or desire for comfort and safety stop us from reaching out to others. We so often celebrate missionaries from previous generations such as James Hudson-Taylor who went to China and founded the China Inland Mission. Hudson-Taylor was seen as a pioneer, being one of the first to go to another nation and seek to be culturally sensitive in what he did. To this end he spoke the local language, wore the national dress, and did all he could to be part of the culture in order to provide the strongest of platforms for the gospel. We celebrate this being done historically or globally, but we also need to make sure we are doing so within our own town and nation at a time when the message can be missed because it feels like we are speaking a foreign language. Philip does this so well with the eunuch.

Philip has already been breaking all kinds of social conventions by leading many Samaritans to Jesus. Now he blows apart further social conventions and barriers by welcoming into the church a eunuch who, according to Jewish law, was not allowed to join (Deuteronomy 23:1).[5] The early church were making it clear in their actions and words that this gospel was not just for the Jews or the privileged, not just for the educated or physically perfect, not just for those who fitted in or were from the right ethnic group, but that this Jesus died for all and his gospel is a message for everyone. Again, this is hugely challenging.

Not long ago we travelled to a church to speak. On the way, we went past a church that had gone to every effort to stop homeless people from sleeping outside their building. There were spikes on the ground, and some fencing and signage making it clear that rough sleepers should stay away. When we arrived at the church for the baptismal service we were ministering at, there was a stark contrast. Instead of people not being welcome there, a homeless man gave his testimony before being baptized. He wasn't just welcome, he was part of the family. The gospel is for everyone.

This was no ordinary eunuch that Philip was encountering. He was a eunuch in the service of Candace, the queen of Ethiopia. He was her treasurer, or in our terms, her chancellor of the exchequer! Once Philip had spoken to him, this man was converted and baptised. This Ethiopian then went on his way rejoicing, unable to keep this newfound joy to himself.[6] As a result of all this, the eunuch then became the first person in history to take the Good News of Jesus to the continent of Africa. Phil Moore puts it this way: 'Because Philip shared the Gospel as the message of Jesus, he saved an Ethiopian eunuch and sent him back to save his nation.'[7]

The official and Philip go their separate ways, but they are now part of the same family and are both carriers of this gospel. John Stott says that the eunuch went on rejoicing 'without the evangelist but with the evangel (Good News), without human aid but with the divine Spirit who gave him joy and courage and power to in his own country preach what he has himself believed.'[8] That should be the same for all of us. Many help in our journey to meeting Jesus and once we have met him we can then have the joy, courage, and power to share about this in the context we are in. Having left the eunuch, Philip also did the same. He went on evangelising, working his way north along the coast preaching through all the towns until he reached Caesarea

This whole chapter in Acts is so incredibly challenging. In human terms it would have made far more sense for Phillip to stay in Samaria, where things were going well and people were responding. However, God has a far better angle on things than we do, and this often means that he possesses different plans for our lives. By the very fact that he's God, if he says go and it doesn't make sense, then we still need to go anyway as he always knows what is best for his people, as well as for the growth of his kingdom.

We Are worthy

For many of us as we think about Philip and the many others in the early church, we can also be prevented from sharing our faith in the same way because we just can't see how we could have the same impact. We might also question our inherent value or intrinsic good in either our actions or ourselves. Low self-esteem, or wrong self-image, is currently posing a massive problem in our church. The same Jesus is with us; the same Spirit empowers us today.

Whenever someone struggles with thinking that they have nothing to offer, our minds often turn to the story of the feeding of the 5,000 in John 6. When you include women and children as well, you discover that there were somewhere between 11,000 and 15,000 hungry people in a field at lunchtime. Jesus asks where they should buy bread (verse 5), and no one knows what to do until Andrew finds a boy's packed lunch and bravely takes it to Jesus.

He can take the little that we have to offer and do things with seemingly inadequate resources that we would never dream to be possible. With Jesus on our side, anything can happen. Here is a boy with five small barley loaves and two small fish, but how far will they go among so many? (verse 9) Andrew can't understand how this small offering will help, but despite his lack of spiritual awareness, he still knows enough to bring it to Jesus. He acknowledges that the packed lunch before him is not even adequate to feed one hungry man, but he is working with a Jesus who works wonders and so he takes it to the King. As a result, Jesus feeds the whole field with plenty to spare. Andrew is probably as surprised as the rest, but he is beginning to realise that this Jesus can take what seem like small efforts to us and use them in incredible ways.

In much the same way, he can take what we have and make it go so much further than we think. The worst thing we can do is keep what we have to ourselves because we don't think it's worth much. We're not sure Philip thought he was the answer to all the eunuch's problems, but he did know who was and pointed the eunuch to, Jesus. In much the same way, we need to realise our worth and play our part.

We are living testimonies of God's grace, not people collecting Hollywood stories.

For this reason, when we think we have nothing to offer, we must still bring it to Jesus. This has the potential to be very exciting. It's fundamental that as a church we start witnessing and living out our faith in every environment that we find ourselves in. We must bring our little and watch Jesus use it amazingly. Just as he took a boy's packed lunch and fed thousands of people, he can take our small efforts and use them in incredible ways.

It is of paramount importance that we avoid beating ourselves up by unfair comparisons. There seem to be some people who just tell amazing stories of leading people to Jesus on trains, in parks, and all over the place. Such tales make the rest of us feel like we can never live up to these standards. Let us be clear on something: we can't.

We met a young woman recently who was feeling really discouraged. She desperately wanted her four college friends to come to faith and none of them were. However, as we probed with questions, it became clear that these four had all been really hostile to Christ a year or so earlier and now, as a result of this girl, they were all no longer hostile though equally not yet all that interested. We turned to the girl and said, 'You should be delighted as your friends are on a journey and you are positively influencing them for Christ even if the progress may seem slow.' We need to celebrate the impact we are making in the everyday not just the kairos moments (the appointment moments in God's plans). All of us today can bring our little to Jesus, and he will use it to help bring others further towards him.

The final great encouragement to us as we seek to do this is one of the most common promises throughout Scripture: that God is with us. This is throughout the Bible, and should help us to be brave. This promise remains with us and, as a result, we can follow him where he leads, share his message with those who are different from us, bring our little to him and be comforted by his unwavering presence.

Yes, but How?

For You:

1 The passion expert said that you can tell what people are passionate about by what they spend their time on, and what they talk about. Think about your life. What would you say are your biggest passions when considering the above?

2 Are you bringing what you have and, like the boy with the packed lunch, offering it to Jesus?

3 What is the Lord doing with your offering? What might he do if your started bringing it to him?

4 Do you want to see him do more? Why not take a moment to ask him to multiply his work through you?

For your group:

1 Philip was operating in a very fruitful space in Samaria. Is it fruitful where you are?

2 In what ways might your church bear more fruit? (Have a look at what is happening in Acts 8.)

3 How would you feel if the Lord called you into the desert? Would you be able to hear him?

4 What does the desert look like for you personally, and for your church collectively?

5 Are there places you feel called into but would rather not go? Why?

6 Philip had no idea what that appointment with one individual would lead to: the gospel going to Africa! Are there individuals in desert places that Jesus is showing you that you need to reach out to?

7 Pray together as a group for bravery and opportunities.

Further Reading:

C. Madavan, *Living on Purpose* (Farnham: CWR, 2018)

F. De Paula, *If not Now, When?* (Watford: Instant Apostle, 2019)

12

Hearing the Voice of God

'Having your spiritual radar up in constant anticipation of His presence—even in the midst of the joyful chaos and regular rhythms of your everyday living—is paramount in hearing God, because sometimes the place and manner you find Him is the least spectacular you'd expect.'

Priscilla Shirer

Being 'unleashed' everywhere starts with a willingness to hear where God might want us to go. It begins with an intimacy with the Lord that means we are able to sense his prompting. Being 'called' involves a surrender of our own agenda and a desperation to see Jesus take over our whole life. Essentially, we crawl onto the altar and allow our life to become an offering for the King because we love him more than we love anything else. We can sometimes want to keep part of our lives from being burnt; we actually want to choose some of our own decisions and to live according to the world's way. The story of Saul becoming Paul, and Ananias being obedient to what the Spirit is saying deeply challenges us. This passage gives us some vital tools and insights into how we embody a church unleashed, the question is will we do an Ananias or will we run and hide? If Ananias had ignored the Lord, history would have looked different, not just for him, but for the entire world: 'If the death and resurrection of Jesus is the hinge on which the great door of history swung open at last, the conversion of Saul of Tarsus was the moment when all the ancient promises of God gathered themselves up, rolled themselves into a ball, and came hurtling through that open door and out into the wide world beyond.'[1]

Yes, we receive the power of the Holy Spirit. We come together to minister in words, works, and wonders, but then we keep on making a choice: will we keep surrendering to and listening to the voice of the Lord or will we turn back to journeying our own way? Are we prepared to allow him to shape things differently to our normal? We were recently having lunch with two of our friends who run a great church in Watford. They were absolutely buzzing with excitment, and we felt our souls lifted by being with them. We asked why they were so happy, and they explained that one New Year's Eve they had stayed in, and had an average time watching pants television. They felt prompted by the Lord to make more of the next year's greeting of a new year, and so instead decided to spend it praying at their church for a mighty move of God in their community in the coming year. They invited others from the church to join them if they fancied, it and over 100 people turned up. We want to hear the Lord in the same way.

Ready for Transformation?

When Saul encounters Jesus on the Damascus road his whole world is transformed inside out, upside down, and back to front. He goes from 'breathing out murderous threats' (9:1) and going to the high priest to ask him for letters so he could take the believers as prisoners (9:2) to quickly 'beginning to preach in the synagogue that Jesus is the son of God' (9:20). Saul was so evil and so far from God, not just in saying horrific things but also going out of his way to act on them. And then Jesus says, 'Why do you persecute me?' Why does he? In his mind he is persecuting the followers of Christ, not Christ himself. Then Saul can no longer see; he can no longer lead; he has to be led. He is totally stopped from continuing the work he was about to do: 'for three days he was blind, and did not eat or drink anything' (9:9). Saul loses his identity, his purpose, his direction, his comrades, his strength, and even his will to live.

We wonder what happens in those three long days. Days of repentance, of being a hermit, of beginning a journey of total transformation. He needed those three days. Like being a caterpillar crawling into a cocoon, he needed to enter that place of darkness to begin to turn into a butterfly. He did not eat anything either—clearly an intense time of fasting to prepare him for what was to come. Working out a call from the Lord involves fasting and sacrifice—it may well happen in a difficult place and perhaps away from what you currently know and love. Some of the journey of transformation and meaning business with God is worked out through laying down what we want and who we want to be to take up who God wants us to be. God refines us during the call: he gets us ready, brings stuff to the surface that he wants us to deal with. You can be sure that if he is doing an intense work in you, he is getting you ready for something.

What happens to you in an encounter with Jesus is so important as to where he is leading you. What he might say to you or do in those moments is unique for your destiny. He never deals with any two people the exact same way. His love has a perfect plan for you and you only. Saul begins to preach 'that Jesus is the Son of God' (9:20). He does not first preach that Jesus saves or loves you or is your friend. Something happened on the Damascus road that made Saul sure that Jesus was who he said he was and now he had to proclaim it. What has God revealed to you in the encounter? Saul knew, and needed to know, that Jesus was truly the Son of God.

When Gavin encountered Christ and gave his life to him, the song 'History Maker' by Delirious was one he sang with all his heart because he knew that the line 'I'm going to be a speaker of truth to all mankind,' was a key part of the call that God had on his life. When Anne was filled with the Spirit she heard the words of the prophet Joel: 'My sons and my daughters will prophesy,' and she knew that in the encounter, part of her role was being made clear. What God reveals in that place of encounter is key for working out your call. He is not interested in making us feel nice without moving us on from where we are. Saul and Ananias were both moved further than they ever would have dreamt.

Calling Changes Our Direction

Our old friend Alex, one of the greatest prophets we have ever known, was riddled with lots of physical struggles, including deafness. When people would ask him if he ever wanted to be healed, Alex would say, 'I'm sure my hearing doesn't get sorted so that I can keep hearing God!' He was so committed to going after God's voice and his agenda over and above the word and way of people.

Saul, as he begins his transformation into Paul, is blind for three days. Not deaf, but blind. Why was this? Yes, the bright light might have momentarily blinded him, but this is a spiritual, supernatural blindness. The purpose of it was not just to shock him with bright light but also to completely and utterly change his direction. He had to be stopped in his tracks in every way and begin to be transformed into new life. He had to change direction. Saul stops seeing what he was seeing and begins to see in a whole new way. His spiritual eyes were turned to truth, to Jesus.

Then we get to this most beautiful bit in Scripture where Saul is filled with the Spirit and something like scales fall from his eyes and he could see again (9:17-18). This is not just a natural seeing; Saul sees a totally new world, a new path—the light and life of Christ has invaded his entire being. A black cloud drops off him, the scales that covered his way drop to the ground. When the Spirit of the Living God comes and fills the children of God, he takes us on a whole new journey, a road to life in all its fullness, and it is not limited to age, gender, social status, or job title. He wants to take us all in a new direction: towards knowing him more, loving him, and serving his broken world.

The Lord wants to enable us to see differently and to have a different perspective. To turn off distraction and head into a new life so that we can know his love and call not just for us, but also for those we love too. The question is, what is blinding us?

We have found it really challenging over the years to keep focused on the call of God over our lives, to keep taking risks, to not get comfortable, to listen for the small, still voice of the Lord. Sometimes we get it wrong, but we hope and pray that our hearts and lives stay mouldable in his hands. It seems that so many people are media driven rather than Jesus-driven, more concerned with their wallpaper rather than anything eternal. We can get so fixated on what we can literally see, rather than what God wants to enable us to see. Our brother, Kris, used to have a t-shirt that read 'He who dies with the most toys, still dies.'

This passage in Acts 9 is a call to consider the road we are traveling on and ask questions about whether we are seeing the right horizon in front of us. Sometimes we are called to take a step that completely changes our direction so that we are never the same again. It may be from darkness to light, from one place to another, one way of thinking to another, or all of the above together.

We are so challenged by the way our friends in the RCCG (Redeemed Christian Church of God) follow the Lord and plant churches. When they begin to sense the Lord leading them to a new area, they send in a team of people to pray for months in that location.

They map out the key institutions and establishments of authorities for prayers, and also walk the streets at odd hours as they fast and pray to seek Jesus, asking that his Holy Spirit would show them where to plant the church, what type of church, and who he is calling them to serve.

These believers are careful not to go to places where there is an already active mission, unless God is calling them to collaborate and work together. They spend time birthing church out of a burden that the presence of God must be re-established where churches have closed down, or where there is no presence of a church or where churches has been replaced by other forms of non-Christian worship.

As God begins to reveal, they begin to be step out and not the other way round. Every single church is born out of a call from the King, and they seek to faithfully step into it.

Their whole focus is on fulfilling the Great Commission: of going into the world to make disciples and not on whether they would choose that destination or how much their salary will be. As a matter of fact, the majority of the churches are birthed out of self-funding fuelled by the passion to see his kingdom come.

Prepared to Get Uncomfortable?

Then we come to Ananias, that poor guy. The Lord calls to him in a vision (9:11). There he is, a faithful follower of Jesus with a terrifying commission. As Tom Wright highlights: 'We know nothing about him except this passage, and it's enough: that he was a believer, that he knew how to listen for the voice of Jesus, that he was prepared to obey it even though it seemed ridiculously dangerous.'[2] This is a man who may have only this mention, but whose life speaks volumes to us about how we should live ours. And then comes the call: 'Go to the house of Judas on Straight Street and ask for a man from Tarsus named Saul, for he is praying' (9:11). You can almost hear the fear rise in Ananias: 'But Lord, no, please no.' He arrests those who believe in you. I know all the bad things he has done. What will happen? What if he hurts me? What if the other believers hear that I have gone to him, and what will they think of me? However, Ananias overcomes his fear and he goes. He believes more in the voice of the Lord than he does in himself. Ananias has the courage to go to the house, proclaim why he is there, pray for healing for Saul's eyes, ask the Spirit to fill him, and baptize him. What a guy!

Incredibly, God changes Ananias so much through this encounter, probably as much as he changes Saul. He would never be the same again after hearing and acting on this word from the throne room. It would build up Ananias' confidence, his faith, his belief in the power of God, and it would remind him that God wanted to use him, that he had a plan for his life as well as everyone else's. At the beginning when the Lord comes to us, we have no idea of the outcome, but if we can overcome fear, we can see amazing things.

We believe that the Lord is longing to move the church away from simply just our business plans and strategies. Planning is important, but we must always be open to changes in the road ahead. He is often longing to take us down a road that we may not have planned or laid out. He is asking his people again if they are willing to get uncomfortable for him, to change direction, to receive instruction that might make them look silly in front of their friends, to overcome their fear, and advance in faith.

How many of our plans start in prayer and with a sense of what the Spirit might be saying, but then get put to one side for a clearer, sensible strategy? How many of us resort to the home in the right place, with a decent pay package and pension plan instead of going after that dream from our youth? None of those things are wrong if God ordains them, but have we even been willing to ponder it? We make decisions every day, but how many are faith-filled decisions and how many are to keep people happy and life smooth? We are so challenged not to fall foul to believing that what we see is the entirety of what God intended, when life in the Spirit is far more of an adventure than we are often prepared to entertain.

We do not want to be those who make a business plan at the expense of a kingdom decision because we cannot trust God with our children, or our churches, or our future. No one would ever have dreamt that Saul would be transformed in such a mighty way, but with God, all things are possible. Yes, we have heads as well as hearts, but the reality that dawns on us through this passage and others in Acts is that calling can come from left field—it may be surprising, scary, unexpected, and demand sacrifice. However, when it comes it will not just transform our lives but the lives of so many others. The question is, are we ready?

The enemy wants to keep us locked in a cycle that leaves no room for discernment. He wants to keep us so busy that we are not able to hear the voice of God when it comes. Ananias had to be still; he needed to be prayerful and intimate with his King to hear him speak like that. Lord, we need that stillness to reign in the British church again. Father, forgive us for filling our time and not seeking your face.

The Acts church were open to the movement of the Holy Spirit, going the way the Counsellor called them to go. Are we, the British church, in danger of losing sight of a call because we have formed hierarchies, job roles, pension plans, and have encouraged people to make sure that they are being treated in a way that they deserve? Have we promoted a view of entitlement at the expense of sacrifice and surrender? Are our roles so defined that they prevent us from moving in step with what the Spirit wants to do? Are we setting up systems that could stop us from moving out of the box and in-line with what the Lord is doing? None of these things named are wrong in and of themselves, but they are if they stop being the vehicles through which the Spirit moves his church and if they hinder the voice of the Lord leading us down another route.

Peter didn't think Cornelius would come to faith but Cornelius did; Peter baptized him and Cornelius received the Holy Spirit. Ananias definitely didn't expect that God would save the murderous Saul, but Jesus met Saul and Saul was converted, so Ananias baptized him and Saul received the Holy Spirit. Philip, when he meets the Ethiopian eunuch, is following the leading of God, even when Philip doesn't understand it. The unexpected happens; the Ethiopian official encounters Christ and is baptised. God is always one step ahead of us. We can trust that he knows what he is doing. We follow his leading, listen to his voice, and lean into his plans, even when we do not fully understand them or cannot work them out. We don't need to understand everything to trust God.

One of our fears is that we become like the Pharisees and are unable to recognize the work of the Lord. Their hearts were in the right place, their motivations were good, but they were dominated by fear rather than by faith, and by preserving the past rather than stepping into the future. The Jewish leaders studied the Scriptures, they had the words of Isaiah, and yet so many of them didn't recognise the Messiah when he came. They were asking the wrong questions, finding distorted answers, and completely missed out on life in all its fullness. Lord, save us from ourselves. That we would remain like clay in the potters' hand, that our hearts would stay soft, and that we would be willing to be unleashed wherever, whatever, and however you require us to be.

Yes, but How?

For you:

1 Ananias was extremely brave going to meet Saul. What would you do if you heard that sort of call?

2 Perhaps you want to hear the voice of God more, even if it is challenging. Why not spend some time asking God to speak to you, to make his voice clearer to you, and then wait. Give space to listen. Turn off all devices and be still.

For your group:

Ananias, Peter, Cornelius, Philip, and Saul all encounter the Lord and his word over their lives, and obediently step the way he is calling. Obedience seems to be one of the key ways that the early disciples witness a powerful move of the Spirit.

1 How obedient are we willing to be?
2 If it meant leaving the safe place?
3 If it meant looking silly?
4 If it meant taking a risk without knowing the outcome?
5 If it meant living by faith?
6 What are we prepared to lay down for the sake of following Jesus?

Do consider this . . . fasting to hear

Two friends of ours that lead a great church near us have started praying and fasting every Monday for breakthrough in the community. Yes, you can fast social media, TV, or chocolate, but when you fast what your body needs to survive, there can be a real impact. There also seems to be a greater connection to the Lord when we fast. Might you consider doing so to petition for breakthrough in your community?

Further Reading:

S. Uppal, *Rouse the Warriors* (Watford: Instant Apostle, 2018)

D. Duncan, *Brave* (Oxford: Monarch Books, 2018)

13

Mission Wider

'The greater danger for most of us lies not in setting our aim too high and falling short; but in setting our aim too low, and achieving our mark.'

Michelangelo

The book of Acts is an incredible account of the life of the early church, but clearly the writer Luke had an awful lot to include and had to be discerning in this. As a result, he is ruthlessly concise when narrating events without immediate significance to the story and the message throughout. However, he was prepared for repetition when recording vitally important events in the life of the early church.[1] The encounter between Peter and Cornelius is so important to Luke that he relates it in full twice (Acts 10 and 11). This is a massive moment in the life of the early church. A huge change is about to take place as it becomes clear that the gospel message of Jesus is for all, not just for a select few who are from the right background and race.

The magnitude of this passage can easily be lost on us today. It is difficult for us to fully understand the impassable gulf in the days of the early church between the Jews and the Gentiles.[2] This was such a huge divide and one that would be unthinkable to cross in the ways that the early church does here. William Barclay writes that 'we usually do not realise how near Christianity was to becoming only another kind of Judaism. All the first Christians were Jews and the whole tradition and outlook of Judaism would have moved them to keep this new wonder to themselves and to believe that God could not possibly have meant it for the despised Gentiles.'[3] Why would God have wanted his family to extend beyond the Jews? This was surely not the plan.

The message of this whole episode is profoundly clear and is repeated several times throughout Acts 10-11 (10:45; 10:46-47; 11:15; 11:17; 11:18). What is this vital message? In short, uncircumcised Gentiles have received the Holy Spirit by faith in Jesus and therefore are entirely equal with the Jewish believers.[4] This is huge. It's like the ultimate cultural heresy. How could the Gentiles possibly be equal to the Jews? This surely could not be right. F. F. Bruce says that it shows that it makes clear, beyond any doubt, that 'God had no favourites. Anyone who feared Him and acted rightly was acceptable to Him, no matter what nation they belonged to. This may be the veriest truism to us, but it was a revolutionary revelation to Peter.'[5]

What a moment this was for all those watching and indeed for Peter. What an interesting time he has had up to this point. He had been brave enough to try walking on the water, but this had ended badly. He had cut off Malchus' ear, causing an almighty distraction at the time of Jesus' arrest. He had been commissioned by Jesus as the alleged rock on which the church will be built, and yet is ashamed of his master and denies him in Luke 22:54-62. Despite all of his failings, Jesus had seen the potential in Peter. Like we tried to do over our many years in youth ministry, Jesus saw in that broken young person someone who could rise up to change the world. Following his restoration on the beach in John 21, the rock was ready to go again. At this stage, Jesus made it clear that he was going to give Peter the keys of the kingdom. The American theologian James Montgomery Boice suggests that Peter was given two keys. The first was to open the door of the gospel to the Jewish people at Pentecost, and the second to open the door of the gospel to the Gentiles when he preached before the Roman centurion Cornelius.[6] What a moment! There were now no longer any barriers to people meeting with the risen Jesus. The gospel was for all.

Public Leadership

Abi Jarvis works with Gavin at the Evangelical Alliance and is passionate about helping people to serve Jesus and impact their surroundings for him wherever they find themselves. She argues that we are all public leaders, as we all influence others, and that we should extend our understanding of mission. The challenge for us today is not like that in Acts where the gospel needs to include more than the Jews. Our challenge is to make sure that the gospel moves out from just our private homes and churches. Abi writes:

How do you act and speak when you're working and living in a culture not your own? According to Acts, you do so in public and guided by the Holy Spirit. Not a bad message for us today! The mission field of the early church wasn't in church buildings. They spoke before, or performed miracles in, crowds of unbelievers (chapters 2, 5, 8, 13, 14, 17, 18, 19, 21, 22, 24). Peter and John spoke before the Sanhedrin (ch 4) and Paul before the Areopagus (ch 7). I wonder what Dionysus said to his fellow Areopagus members following his conversion (ch 17). Did it affect his attitude to council business?

Too often today faith is relegated to the private spaces of home or church. Even though the law protects Christians' right to speak about their faith we are fearful of our reception. We don't explain that our work ethics are inspired by Jesus' teaching. We turn down media opportunities in case we're pigeonholed as out of date. And who would want to admit to being an evangelical Christian on Twitter?

We have the right to bring our faith into our leadership—it's a core part of our identity. And it's necessary to truly be salt and light, as Jesus called us to be (Matthew 5:13-16). We can also have confidence that, like the early church, the Holy Spirit will guide our words and actions if we ask for it. The Spirit provides wisdom, discernment and courage to Jesus' followers and nothing could be more important for public leaders. In fact, the Spirit was a leadership requirement for the seven men who distributed food to widows (6:3).

The Spirit will fill us as we speak before authorities and crowds, just as it filled Peter and Stephen (4:8, 6:10), and will guide our steps as it guided Philip to the Ethiopian eunuch (8:29). I imagine the businesswoman Lydia (ch 16) Spirit-filled as she led her workers and engaged with her competitors. The Spirit can give us a prophetic voice into social concerns, as it brought prophecy of an empire-world famine (11:28). I wonder what words the Spirit gave to Tabitha, a community leader (ch 9), as she ran her enterprise.

Public leaders must 'live by the Spirit' in order to be free of 'flesh desires' (so often the downfall of leaders who separate their faith from their leadership) and instead receive the fruit of the Spirit—'love, joy, peace, forbearance, kindness, goodness, faithfulness, gentleness and self-control' (Galatians 5:16-22). When we do so, the Spirit will guide our actions and our words and only God knows what opportunities this may bring.

So have confidence and courage to follow the example of Jesus' first followers, to speak in public settings and lead with the guidance of the Holy Spirit. And like the church in Acts, stay connected to one another in mutual support as you represent Jesus in your different mission fields.

What About the Wider Culture?

We all need to play our part individually, but we also have a corporate calling as the people of God to transform the culture of the nation. So what would it really take for an unleashed church to impact and reach every area of the nation for Christ today? American writer Os Hillman identifies seven key areas of influence 'business, government, media, arts and entertainment, family, education and the church.'[7] Other Christians have talked about this in terms of 'spheres' or 'frontlines'. We as Christians need to be influencing, or better still, leading, within these seven areas. We can't afford to just stick to church, for that is but one of the seven. In order to transform our communities, and moreover our nation, we need Christians making a difference in each of these places. We're not talking about imposing Christianity on society, but seeking ways to do good to all and be a blessing to the world.

We as church need to learn to support people in these other areas too. It's easy to know what's needed to support an overseas missionary with their financial needs and regular prayer letters, but how do we as Christians help business leaders living for Christ? How can we stop bemoaning the methods of the media and instead infiltrate them? Arts and entertainment are fields that desperately need Christian presence, and as for family and education, these are historically real strongpoints for the church. Why shouldn't the next England football captain be a Christian? In our local congregations we wonder how many different cultural spheres are represented in our churches and how well we are doing at supporting people in these areas. We must start validating, endorsing, and supporting people seeking to bring the light and love of Christ into environments of influence beyond the walls of the church. Beyond the barriers we have put in place.

So as well as the areas of influence, what kind of people are needed in order to make real change? What constitutes a game changer? In his book *The Catalyst Leader,* Brad Lomenick outlines eight characteristics that are required to become a changemaker. These are: (1) *Calling* (finding out God's unique plan for your life); (2) *Authenticity* (being the person you are meant to be at all times and sharing this with others); (3) *Passion* (for life and your relationship with God); (4) *Capable* (growing your gift set and being up to achieving high standards); (5) *Courageous* (learning to push through and take risks. Being able to manage your fears and not be stopped by them.);

(6) *Principled* (based in clearly held views and principles); (7) *Hopeful* (optimistic about a brighter future); and (8) *Collaborative* (someone who will work with others towards the greater good).[8]

We must fight to establish our Lord's relevance and stop an increasingly secularized world from forgetting who Jesus is. We can all do this. We can all be salt and light in our own environments. We all have colleagues, neighbours, and friends that the church may struggle to impact through any other means than us. Therefore, let's get active. As two famous lines from *The Chronicles of Narnia* say, 'Aslan is on the move' and 'He's not a tame lion.' God is doing great things, and we need to play our part and join with him. He is active and desires to use us to fulfil his purposes in our environments. Mark Greene puts it this way: 'God is at work. And God has been at work in his people, in his church, in this land. And, no doubt, in you, in a myriad ways. We may not get to see the outcome in our lifetimes, but it is so. And so, the Lord be with you, whatever hat you wear. The Lord be with you on your frontline.'[9]

It is certainly not all about the church and its buildings. We need to be involved in society on every level and in each environment. It's about us as Christians taking responsibility—knowing that we speak and act under the authority of God. It means caring about the place where God has put us, and stepping up, speaking out, and engaging in public life. Taking our place in politics, the media, and all parts of society. Bringing about change in his name.

This happens in so many different ways. We all have a chance to witness and need to take these opportunities. We, Gavin and Anne, are both big football fans. Gavin passionately follows AFC Wimbledon and Anne follows Liverpool. When the Reds picked up their sixth Champions League trophy on June 1, 2019, there was an amazing moment where the Liverpool goalkeeper, Alisson Becker, threw off his club goalie top to reveal a homemade patter on a T-shirt below. It was a drawing of the cross and then an equals sign and a heart. He then deliberately sat at the front of the podium so the whole world would see his evangelistic message as the team celebrated that Jesus died on the cross as an act of love for all people.[10]

The next morning Gavin tweeted the photo with the following message: 'Delighted for @AnneCalver that @LFC won the @ChampionsLeague, but even happier to see their goalkeeper, @Alissonbecker, giving all the glory to Jesus. We British Christians have a lot to learn from our South American brothers and sisters about not being ashamed of the Gospel!' Within half an hour the goalkeeper himself tweeted Gavin back with '@GavCalver God is love!!' Within hours, Gavin's tweet had received over 3000 likes and hundreds of retweets, and the message got out still further. What an incredible thing Alisson did in pointing the glory to Jesus in his greatest moment of human triumph. He had been taught well; the dynamic and gifted Liverpool manager, Jürgen Klopp, is equally clear that his Christian faith has taught him there is far more to life than winning trophies.[11]

Wherever we find ourselves, that place is where we can make a difference for Christ. Where we can be unleashed. As the bride of Christ, let's take up this call to be mobilized into action, to realize our ambition of touching a small part of our world for Jesus on our own unique context. We must believe that our part is worthwhile and wherever we find ourselves—from the classroom, to the workplace, to the family dinner table, to the nightclub, or the football pitch—we need to share something of the story of Jesus. Every one of us has a unique part to play in reaching the world with this incredible good news. Let each of us make sure that we play it.

Impacting Our Cultural Spheres

As well as the seven overall areas of culture there are many subgroups within these categories too. We all have areas of influence where we can make a difference. But what would it take to infiltrate a cultural frontline for Christ? Here our friend Simon Barrington looks at this from the perspective of business:

There is a widespread view that the Church has nothing to say to business and that Christians regard business—certainly in terms of the generation of profit—as inherently bad. That God and business simply don't mix and that competition in the marketplace is essentially incompatible with Christian values. It's easy for us as Christians to consider our witness as being irrelevant in the commercial environment, that we have nothing relevant and certainly nothing prophetic to say. But our conviction is that there is a way in which God has designed business to work, a way that brings a wholeness, a depth of relationship and an authenticity that enables businesses to be more sustainable, more transparent, more holistic and more relevant.

And the environment in business is changing and waking up to these realities: that the current system is broken and is not working. Frederick Laloux, a mainstream Business author who has a huge following, in his book, *Re-inventing Organisations*, describes the future of business as being (1) wholehearted, (2) purposeful, and (3) self-managed.[12] This new way of working recognizes the change in the order of 'seeking' in our lives. Recognition, success, wealth, and belonging are no longer the primary things that are sought after. Rather, 'we pursue a life well-lived, and the consequences might just be recognition, success, wealth, and love.'

In this context, the new watchwords of business are relationship, honesty, integrity, authenticity, sustainability, wholeness, and purpose. This is particularly true in the millennial generation. The door is wide open for the church to engage—and it is engaging. Take, for example, ministry2business in Manchester, led by Reverend Pete Horlock. Pete and his team are focussed on supporting Christians in the workplace, providing mentoring, support, and networking to bring an authentic Christian voice to businesses across the city. Their vision is of a city transformed, of businesses transformed, of professionals and businesses in the city finding their place in the mission of God.

One of the challenges is the secular/sacred divide that has existed for generations. Many church leaders have little knowledge of where their congregations spend most of their week. But that is changing. One church in Ipswich is huddling leaders on a Zoom/Skype call on a Thursday lunchtime, allowing them to be discipled and supported in the workplace.

Others are going further and seeking to bring a more relational approach to business. For example the Relationships Foundation in Cambridge, is working with organisations to improve the quality of relationship in boardrooms—with customers, with suppliers, and with employees—believing that business is better when organisations not only steward people and finances, but also the relationships at their heart.

In the realm of leadership, Forge Leadership recently ran a Lead Honestly event in the University of Suffolk that attracted leaders of all faiths and to talk about how leaders can be more authentic, vulnerable, and honest; and how they can look after their own wellbeing and lead with passion and conviction.
It's time for the Church to engage with business.

This is just one of the many areas where Christians can make a difference. As the church in the UK, it's time we started engaging more effectively with them all and extending our view as to what our mission field really is.

Gospel for All

When the restrictions as to whom the gospel was made available to were powerfully stripped away in the book of Acts, a statement was made to all the generations of the church to follow: the gospel is for all. We need to make sure that we are not restricting the message from anyone and that no one is excluded from the opportunity to hear and respond to the life-giving gospel message. The great author Max Lucado says, 'God loves you just the way you are, but he refuses to leave you there. He wants you to be just like Jesus.'[13] The gospel is for all, but that doesn't mean that when we meet Jesus we don't change. We are regularly encouraged by encounters with friends from before we knew Jesus who are amazed at who we are today. When we meet Jesus and surrender our lives for him, so much then changes.

We, the UK church, need to take away the lessons from Acts and live them out in our context. We are in a spiritual battle for the nation, and we must not let Satan stop us in our efforts to reach others with the gospel. Phil Moore puts it this way:

If you learn the lessons of the book of Acts, Satan has only one option left to prevent you from wreaking massive damage on his kingdom. He must make you shortsighted, and trick you into limiting the scope of your ministry for Christ. If he can restrict your gaze to Sundays, he will. If he can turn it into private religion, or even corporate church religion, he will do that too. If he can dupe you into ring-fencing your faith away from work colleagues, relatives, neighbours or any of the many people groups in your nation, he still hopes to carry the day. We mustn't let him. Every limit, restriction, and barricade of Satan must be broken for the sake of Jesus' Gospel.[14]

Yes, but How?

For you:

We mentioned Brad Lomenick's eight characteristics required to become a changedmaker (page 114). Why not look down this list and spend a short time thinking about where you are personally with each one.

1 Calling – Do you know God's plan for your life?
2 Authenticity – Are you being truly, honestly, yourself?
3 Passion – How passionate are you for God and for the life he longs for you to lead?
4 Capable – Are you growing in the gifts he has given you? How might you grow them more?
5 Courageous – Where are you taking risks? What might be stopping you? How can you overcome your fears?
6 Principled – What clear views, values, and principles do you hold to?
7 Hopeful – Are you hopeful over the future? In what ways?
8 Collaborative – Who are you working and journeying with? Who might you need to start doing this with?

For your group:

Finding your frontline

LICC has put together resources on finding your 'frontline'—the place where you spend much of your time, where you meet people who don't know Jesus. Their Life on the Frontline course is designed to help each other make a difference for Christ in these places. See: https://www.licc.org.uk/ourresources/lifeonthefrontline/ Which area (or subgroup) do you have an influence in?

1 Business
2 Government

3 Media
4 Arts and entertainment
5 Education
6 Family
7 Religion

How can you take Jesus into your area of influence?
Through conversation, through action, through prayer?
What is he asking you to do? Remember that you join with thousands of brothers and sisters seeking to show the love of Jesus and taking his truth into the places that they influence.

Public Leadership

You could run the SENT course. It is a new course to help churches equip public leaders in their congregations to be transformational in their workplace and local community.

If you have leaders in your church involved in education, health, politics, business, the arts and media, or any other area of public life, help them to be transformational in their places of work and their community.

SENT is designed for churches to use with small groups of public leaders in order to think, discuss, and pray about what it means to be Christian public leaders.

More info here: https://www.eauk.org/resources/what-we-offer /courses-and-small-groups/sent

You could join the Public Leader training course, which seeks to equip emerging leaders who are passionate about growing in their Christian public leadership.

Designed for Christian public leaders in their twenties and thirties, it's a journey of equipping, mentoring, and supporting public leaders to grow into their unique roles of leadership wherever they've been called. Over the course, the public leaders grow in confidence to use their Christian voice in their workplaces and communities. The course runs in Northern Ireland, Scotland, Wales, and England.

More info here: https://www.eauk.org/what-we-do/initiatives /public-leadership/public-leadership-course

Further Reading:

B. Lomenick, *The Catalyst Leader* (Nashville: Thomas Nelson Inc., 2013)

M. Greene, *Thank God It's Monday* (Milton Keynes: Scripture Union, 2001)

Part 5

UNLEASHED PARTICIPATORS

Acts 12:1–17

Acts 12:1-17

Peter's Miraculous Escape From Prison

It was about this time that King Herod arrested some who belonged to the church, intending to persecute them. ²He had James, the brother of John, put to death with the sword. ³When he saw that this met with approval among the Jews, he proceeded to seize Peter also. This happened during the Festival of Unleavened Bread. ⁴After arresting him, he put him in prison, handing him over to be guarded by four squads of four soldiers each. Herod intended to bring him out for public trial after the Passover.

⁵So Peter was kept in prison, but the church was earnestly praying to God for him.

⁶The night before Herod was to bring him to trial, Peter was sleeping between two soldiers, bound with two chains, and sentries stood guard at the entrance. ⁷Suddenly an angel of the Lord appeared and a light shone in the cell. He struck Peter on the side and woke him up. 'Quick, get up!' he said, and the chains fell off Peter's wrists.

⁸Then the angel said to him, 'Put on your clothes and sandals.' And Peter did so. 'Wrap your cloak around you and follow me,' the angel told him. ⁹Peter followed him out of the prison, but he had no idea that what the angel was doing was really happening; he thought he was seeing a vision. ¹⁰They passed the first and second guards and

came to the iron gate leading to the city. It opened for them by itself, and they went through it. When they had walked the length of one street, suddenly the angel left him.

[11] Then Peter came to himself and said, "Now I know without a doubt that the Lord has sent his angel and rescued me from Herod's clutches and from everything the Jewish people were hoping would happen."

[12] When this had dawned on him, he went to the house of Mary, the mother of John, also called Mark, where many people had gathered and were praying. [13] Peter knocked at the outer entrance, and a servant named Rhoda came to answer the door. [14] When she recognized Peter's voice, she was so overjoyed she ran back without opening it and exclaimed, 'Peter is at the door!'

[15] 'You're out of your mind,' they told her. When she kept insisting that it was so, they said, 'It must be his angel.'

[16] But Peter kept on knocking, and when they opened the door and saw him, they were astonished. [17] Peter motioned with his hand for them to be quiet and described how the Lord had brought him out of prison. 'Tell James and the other brothers and sisters about this,' he said, and then he left for another place.

14

Peter's Miraculous Escape

'Prayer should be the key of the day and the lock of the night.'

George Herbert

Acts chapter 12 is one of the most exciting and terrifying moments in Scripture. The pain and yet the joy of what Peter must have experienced from being stripped, chained, and imprisoned to being woken by an angel, set free, and able to return to the believers is a story we think of as confined to the history books or perhaps only happening on the other side of the world.

And yet the same God who does this is the one who wants to transform his church today. We don't want these kinds of stories to only be read or heard about, but to actually be happening right here in the UK. Granted, we would rather not have the persecution, but we do long to see a move of God that is so incredible, even the angels are actively involved.

One of the questions we have been praying and asking is, 'Lord, show us what we need to learn from your word; what is it about this story of Peter's miraculous escape from prison that we need to take note of if we want to be a church unleashed in the power of the Holy Spirit, witnessing miracles like this?'

The first thing we notice is the reality of the believers praying. If you read again the words in verses 5 and 12 of chapter 12 in Acts, we hear that the 'church was earnestly praying to God for him [Peter]' and 'where many people had gathered and were praying.' This idea of earnestness comes from the idea of hands stretched out and hearts wide open, crying out to God for breakthrough. It is wholehearted, urgent petitioning. Peter is asleep in prison in the night, and at the same time, the church is active and engaged in prayer for his release.[1] This incredible narrative of escape from prison is completely covered in prayer, and this is not just any kind of prayer, it is passionate, it involves lots of people praying together, and it didn't last for just an hour—it went on, and on and on. James Montgomery Boice points out that this was not just any prayer meeting. This gathering had four clear qualities: they were praying to God, they were praying together, they were praying earnestly, and they were praying specifically.[2] Not a bad blueprint for any prayer gathering!

Would the angel have come and set Peter free if the believers hadn't been praying? Could he have? Yes, of course, but would he have released him? We know one hundred percent that the prayers of the saints transform lives and situations.

Prayer is incredibly exciting. It is the most dynamic, life-changing, weapon that we hold in our hands, and yet so often we underrate and devalue what prayer can do. When I, Anne, was out in Turkey ministering amongst the Iranian believers, there would be a prayer meeting before the service. Someone would say, 'Right everyone, it's time to pray' (well not quite like that because it was in Farsi, but you get the idea), and every single person would begin to pray passionate, heart-felt prayers, all together right from their guts, as if their whole life depended on it. I was so taken aback when I first heard their cries because what was so apparent was that their relationship with Jesus was so real, genuine, and life changing.

After a while I began to wonder if their prayers would end—some were on their knees, others lifting their hands, and the presence of the Almighty was tangible in that small packed room. I checked my watch like a good Brit does, concerned that we were running late to begin the service and people would be waiting. I honestly don't know why I sweated over it because when we finally entered the main hall, the meeting had just begun without us. People were publicly reading the Scripture and beginning to spontaneously worship. We just joined in.

We reckon that this prayer in Acts 12, and throughout the Book of Acts, is a bit like the prayer time I witnessed at the Iranian church: somewhere you wanted to be because you knew that the prayers were going to change the atmosphere and make a dent in the universe. It was also prayer that was more important than anything else because it was driven and empowered by the Holy Spirit, so much so that people weren't distracted by anything else.

God's house is a house of prayer (Isaiah 56:7; Matthew 21:13; Mark 11:13) corporately and individually, and without it we might as well go our separate ways. The Lord launched his church off the back of the prayers of his followers, and the reason is because everything flows from him and then it can be released through us. Our relationship with him is at the heart of our faith, and if believers throughout history have no relationship, then there is no prayer and we are not truly building his church.

We believe that God wants us to be ready for what he is going to do by the power of his Holy Spirit, and this begins in prayer. God wants to give his children visions, dreams, prophetic words, and pictures. He wants to pour out refreshing rain into our souls. He longs to draw us to a place of repentance so that we might deal with issues we have with others. He wants to draw out gifts in people and heal the broken and draw the lost and set the captive free. Where does all of this start? In prayer. Because that's where God begins to speak to us. The question is, are we expecting him too?

If you think about it, the most significant life-changing events in your life have prayer at the heart. At an Alpha Holy Spirit day twenty years ago, we were praying and a man got up and said, 'There is a girl here and God is saying, "it's Bible college, it's definitely Bible college."' I, Anne, collapsed to my knees and began to weep. I had no idea what Bible college was, but I knew the word was for me. Looking back now, those few words, heard and responded to in prayer, changed my entire life in the most incredible way

The people of God were praying for Peter and something

incredible began to happen. This is a really miraculous moment. As one theologian puts it, here we have 'a divine intervention by a supernatural visitant.'³ Wow! An angel of the Lord comes and strikes Peter on the side to wake him up (12:7). This is not a very nice wake-up call is it? An alarm clock is bad enough, never mind being struck on the side. At least it was by an angel!

There is an incredible sense of urgency here in the narrative: 'Quick, get up!' Peter is naked, asleep in chains with guards on either side, and then suddenly woken and moved. He gets dressed and he gets led out.

Hang on a second—there is something not to be missed here. God wants to wake his children up urgently for what he wants them to do.

The question then is, are we sleeping? In a dark cave, chained up, asleep—is that a picture of where the church is right now? If it is, or even if it challenges us a little bit, then how do we wake up? We do not want to miss what the Lord is going to do through his children.

Out running a short time ago, I, Anne, saw a very large pigeon in the road. The bird was struggling to flap its wings and fly because it had consumed so much. As it wobbled its huge weight across the road, I began to hear a car heading our way. Instead of just taking to the air like a normal pigeon would do, it stayed on its feet and tried desperately to move towards the pavement. Thankfully, it managed to edge itself into the side of the road and the car sped past, avoiding it by a few centimetres. Now I'm not a big fan of pigeons and living in London I do not rejoice in their increasing numbers; they are like rats with wings. However, I continued on my way, grateful that it was safe and wondering how it had gotten so fat that it could not fly.

The bird had eaten so much (no doubt munching stuff it is not designed to eat) that it could no longer do what it was designed to do: fly. It struck me that there are things that we are doing and perhaps stuff that we are eating that the Lord never wanted us to do or have. Or maybe in small doses they are okay, but in our consumer culture we have been led down a road of indulgence that has made us so comfortable and set in our ways that we can no longer rise and fly. I don't believe the Lord, the author of our life, ever designed us to see the narrow perspective of the road that that pigeon could see. He designed us to soar into life in all its fullness and to have a greater supernatural perspective on the world we live in. The king of kings does not want us to be sucked into a cycle of living like the rest of the western world, but to be set apart as children of God in a crooked and depraved generation.

The questions the Lord has been putting to us and the conviction that we have known in our hearts is: what are we consuming that is stopping us from doing all that the Lord has for us? What is making us so fat in the world that we are unable to soar and rise to the potential that Jesus has for us in the power of his Holy Spirit?

Proverbs 23:19-21 contains some provocative words: 'Listen my son and be wise, and keep your heart on the right path. Do not join those who drink too much wine or gorge themselves on meat, for gluttons and drunkards become poor, and drowsiness clothes them in rags.' Now we don't quote this to necessarily highlight wine and meat, but to highlight the word 'drowsiness'. There are some things that we are doing that are making us sleepy—there is a thick cultural cloud obliterating our vision of what God is calling us to and all that he is longing to say.

We need the angel of the Lord to come and wake us up. To lead us out of darkness—out of sin, distraction, busyness, and oppression. Light shines into the cell (Acts 12:7a) and then the chains fall off Peter's wrists (12:7b). Wow! Not only does an angel come, but then this happens. And then there is more: the guarded iron gate opens for them all by itself (12:10)! Peter is in darkness, he is guarded on every side, he is naked and in chains and then led out of all of it! Can you picture this? Imagine you are Peter in that cell. Imagine the fear in the darkness, the pain around your wrists, the shame, and then being led past all those guards to freedom. Incredible.

God wants to transform our lives—he is longing to breathe light into our darkness, to set us free from our chains, and take us by the hand into freedom.

It's fascinating how the angel comes to Peter in his darkest moment, wakes him, frees him, and leads him out of the worst danger and struggle but then departs (12:10). Perhaps what the Lord wants his children to know is the truth that he really does send his angels to attend to us in the most challenging times. Think of Jesus in the desert for forty days being tempted: 'He was with the wild animals, and angels attended him' (Mark 1:13). Remember Shadrach, Meshach, and Abednego in the fiery furnace? King Nebuchadnezzar sees that they are not being burnt alive and states, 'Look! I see four men walking around in the fire, unbound and unharmed, and the fourth looks like a son of the gods' (Daniel 3:25). We might feel alone and desperate, but the truth is a bit like this line from the poem 'Footprints in the Sand': 'During the times of most trial and suffering, it is then that he carries us.'

We wonder what keeps us in chains. What makes us feel like we are in darkness and unable to be free? I, Anne, remember praying with a girl at a summer conference who was deeply struggling with anorexia. She hated herself and what she was doing, but was finding it impossible to stop hurting herself. A friend and I sat down to minister to her, and as she sought the Lord's forgiveness for the way she viewed herself and began to receive his mighty love and truth into her heart and life, I could visibly see chains breaking in her body. The ministry went on for a couple of hours as she found freedom. At the end of our time together, I could see no more chains, just a relaxed young girl with peace filling her soul.

A year later I was eating lunch in the team dining area at the same conference, and this bouncing girl, grinning from ear to ear, came up to me, her hands laden with crumble and custard. She spilled out, 'Anne, do you remember me?' I looked at her curiously. I didn't recall. 'It's me! The girl you prayed with last year to get healed from anorexia. God did it, Anne. I have been well ever since! Now I am here to serve on team and share my story with other young people.' I stood there in shock as joy came rushing over me. 'Praise Jesus!' I said.

Our God wants to transform lives. The enemy will do anything he can to keep you where you are and prevent the walk to freedom. Some of us look out from where we are and all we see are hurdles—like the soldiers and the gate in the passage—and we think it is impossible to get free. God shows us that when he moves his powerful hand, nothing can stand in his way. It was true then, and it is true today.

The final thing that almost hilariously jumps out from this passage is that Peter doesn't believe he is actually being set free even though it is happening to him (12:9). F. F. Bruce puts it this way: 'Peter's amazed by it all, not realising that it was really taking place, but suspecting that it was all a dream, and that he would soon find himself with the soldiers in the cell, compelled to face whatever the morning might bring.'[4] What an incredible thing that even Peter thought this was too miraculous to be reality. The believers don't believe it is happening either. Look at verses 14-15. 'Peter is at the door!' Rhoda says. 'You are out of your mind,' they told her. 'It must be his angel,' they say. Peter has to keep on knocking! Even though they have been praying like mad for Peter's release, here they are not believing it is happening. They assume that it is an angel. The Jews believed that people had guardian angels, and the disciples assume that is what this must be.[5] But this is not an angel; it is Peter. Oh, that we don't have our own 'Rhoda moments' today. That we can avoid the challenge of praying fervently for something and then missing the answer to our prayers even if they are just behind the door.

Tom Wright puts it like this: 'I find this strangely comforting: partly because Luke is allowing us to see the early church for a moment not as a great bunch of heroes and heroines of the faith, but as the same kind of muddled, half-believing, faith-one-minute-and-doubt-the-next sort of people as most Christians we all know.'[6]

Do we really believe that God can and wants to answer our

prayers? Those things that we have been praying and longing for—do we need to raise our faith again to believe that God can move mountains? Are we expecting miracles and transformation or has our culture made us doubtful? We really believe that the Lord wants to add wonders to our prayers. It might be that your answer is, like Peter, waiting just outside the door. All you have to do is open it. Sometimes this takes bravery though. John Stott points out that when Peter knocked at the door 'the praying group must immediately have imagined that they had received a visit from the secret police.'[7] The disciples were scared and waited in suspense, unaware of the fact that the answer to their prayers was standing outside the door.

An unleashed church is a church that begins to pray like they have never prayed before, individually and corporately. It is a church that wakes up to the world it is in and seeks to look, sound, and smell different to it. It is a church that starts on its knees in confession and rises through shaking off the chains that seek to pin it down. A church that starts believing for so much more than what we currently see, and begins to step out trusting God to come through in every place we set our feet, for his glory.

The Cost of Being Unleashed for Some

Henrietta Blyth is the CEO of Open Doors UK. Here she writes powerfully about what it means to be an unleashed church today for some of our brothers and sisters around the world in nations that persecute Christians. Here she writes specifically about a situation in Bangladesh.

They are saying they will cut us and 'have a bath in our blood. This is not a line from a dystopian Hollywood film, but what I was told by Gaus when I was in Bangladesh last July. When her Muslim family discovered that she and her husband and daughter were devout Christians, this was their reaction.

Gaus found out about the Bible and Jesus from her husband-to-be when she was only 13 years old. Gaus's sister found her reading the New Testament and burnt it. 'I went crazy,' Gaus told me. 'But whatever was inside my heart, she could not burn that.'

When her mother and sisters discovered that she had been secretly married in a church two years later, they tied Gaus to the veranda of the house by her hair and beat her with bamboo until she could no longer stand. In the end, her father rescued her by cutting off her hair at the nape of her neck with a knife. She and her husband escaped and now run a Bible school funded by an Open Doors partner and also offer shelter to other Christians who have been forced to flee.

Just like the new believers in Acts, Christians in Bangladesh are significantly in the minority (less than 0.5%). The vast majority of Bangladeshis are Muslim (89%). In theory, it is a secular country, but it is number forty-eight on Open Doors' World Watch List of the fifty most dangerous countries for Christians. The Qu'ran states that anyone who converts from Islam to another religion is an infidel and brings shame on their family. If the family kills them, this will return honour to them. Many Bangladeshi Muslims are coming to Christ, and they worship in secret and at risk of their lives.

In Matthew 10:36 Jesus said, 'A man's enemies will be the members of his own household.' This is exactly what is happening in Bangladesh right now. We heard story after story of Christians being persecuted by their own parents, siblings, and other family members.

When Karim's family discovered he had become a Christian, they bound him by a chain all night. His father and oldest brother said they would kill him and hang his body in a public place. Five hundred local people came to take him from his in-laws' home on Christmas morning, but a friend helped him to escape.

Mehedi's cousin is a sub-inspector of police. Before the last Eid festival, he found Mehedi reading a Bible in the family home. He snatched it and began to rip it apart. Then he grabbed a broom and told the family to beat him. Mehedi told us, 'I was praying and crying, "Lord, don't allow him to throw my Bible in the river or somewhere else."'

Mehedi was forced out of the family home and now lives nearby. His family are ashamed and beg him, 'Please come back to Islam.' His policeman cousin even offered to give him a job with a hefty salary if he would just abandon his faith. But Mehedi is standing strong.

In Matthew 10:37 Jesus continued, 'Anyone who loves his father or mother more than me is not worthy of me; anyone who loves his son or daughter more than me is not worthy of me; and anyone who does not take his cross and follow me is not worthy of me. Whoever finds his life will lose it, and whoever loses his life for my sake will find it.'

Gaus, Karim, and Mehedi have lost everything to follow Jesus—because they know that he is worth infinitely more than anybody or anything else.

Perhaps it's time for us to follow their example.

Yes, but How?

For you:

1 Do you feel like you are flying in your faith at the moment or are you hobbling along like that pigeon? Why?
2 How is your prayer life? Do you love spending time with Jesus?
3 Why not take some time telling the Lord where you long to be, what you long to see, and where you want him to take you.

For your group:

1 What does corporate prayer look like in your church? Is it a power-house of prayer?
2 Are decisions made out of a place of prayer? Significant moves of God always have prayer at the very core.
3 Would you describe yourself, and the Christians in your life, as being alert to what the Lord is doing in your workplaces, school gates, streets? How can we be more aware?
4 What are the chains restricting people at the moment? How can you pray into them, asking the Lord to liberate his children?
5 Is it time to believe for more?

Further Reading:

P. Greig, *How to Pray: A Simple Guide for Normal People* (London: Hodder & Stoughton, 2019)
D. Green, *Mountain Moving Prayer: The Unlimited Potential* (London: SPCK, 2019)

15

Unleashed to Unleash

'For to be free is not merely to cast off one's chains, but to live in a way that respects and enhances the freedom of others.'

Nelson Mandela

I, Anne, found myself in a curled-up heap on the floor of a solitary confinement cell 6 ft. by 8 ft. in size. As I looked up with tears streaming down my face, I began to read the scriptures etched into the wall. The space I found myself in broke me to pieces. I shifted to my knees and began to pray.

This was not how I planned to react when I visited the 'mock-up' cell at the Elam stand at a conference. Friends had encouraged me to go and see it to experience what it is like for our persecuted brothers and sisters in the Evin Prison in Iran. Entering the small dark cell with the door shut behind me, something shifted in my guts. People were queuing, waiting for an opportunity to see what the makeshift cell was like, but their wait would be longer than what I had planned. You see, God got hold of my heart in that small dark space, and I knew that there was something he wanted me to understand about following him: my western world view and my faith was not like those of the people locked up all over the world for Jesus—I wasn't even sure it was strong enough to warrant a prison sentence.

For a while after that experience, plus another couple of interesting encounters, I was left trying to piece together what the Spirit was saying to me. I spoke to David, the head of Elam, and began to ask questions about ministering amongst Iranians. His third invitation was the one that got me: 'Anne, how about you head out to minister in Turkey to the Iranian churches, and if it makes any difference to your decision, the churches are overseen by the lady whose cell you wept in.' The next piece of the puzzle began to unfold and, a bit like Philip with the Ethiopian eunuch, I needed to go out on a limb to an unknown place to see his kingdom at work in the wider church.

The reason we include this story, and we will unpack it a bit more, is because God was planting seeds for this book and beginning to speak to us about what a church unleashed looks like. You see, the Iranian church felt like the Acts church. Out in Turkey the Lord was adding to their number, daily, people who were being saved. The Lord was showing us a picture of something and asking us to pay attention: Iranian Christians are carrying revival; they are filled with the Holy Spirit and unleashed everywhere together in words, works, and wonders.

Being amongst a large number of Iranians in Turkey kept bringing tears to my, Anne's, eyes, because it is what we long to see in the UK. They are living with everything for Jesus. Perhaps they do feel afraid of imprisonment, and yes, they do live with pain over separation from family and long for their country. However, they know Jesus is alive in such a powerful way that their boldness keeps them proclaiming the gospel—demonstrating it through words, works, and wonders—and living with a certainty that heaven is their ultimate home. The Iranian Christians that I, Anne, have had the privilege of meeting and ministering with are alive in a way that we long to see across the church in our nation.

Church is not an hour and a half on a Sunday and nothing more. Fellowship is not one meeting from 8-9:30 p.m. on an evening a week, if work allows. Services don't just go through the motions without wonders present. There is no dispute over when to do the next evangelism course. Volunteers are not burnt out serving the observers.

Right at the heart of everything was prayer, and it was happening all the time. The love of God at work amongst the body of believers was so real you could almost touch it, and so infectious you could not ignore or shrug it off. There was no 'effort' to do something or see something happen, there was just 'longing' and 'hunger.'

The Lord was saying 'Look.' Now look again. Keep looking. He drew attention to the fact that everyone was participating, using different gifts, selfless, without hierarchy, and were committed to Jesus first and then one another to the point of being willing to lay down their lives. I wept again.

Now do hear us clearly: there are aspects of this that we witness in our churches here in the UK—there are definitely signs of life. However, the overriding sense that we live with is that Jesus longs to move by his Holy Spirit not just in Iran, Turkey, China, North Korea, etc., but throughout the world. He is coming back for his bride, and he needs his bride to make herself ready. He wants to wake us up from our slumber, liberated from chains, and move as one in freedom and power.

Just recently we heard how the Lord is moving amongst the Iranian people, not just in Turkey, Armenia, and Iran, but right here in the UK. Seven years ago two Iranians turned up at a church in the East Midlands, and now 135 people have been baptised and 538 have been saved! The rapid spread of the gospel amongst the Iranians in that area has now begun to spill out into the Afghan and Kurdish communities too with many of them beginning to come to faith in Jesus. We are certain that this is one of many other stories in the UK where Iranian people are carrying revival into our communities. More, Lord! We long to see it in every nation, people group, age, and church denomination.

Break Free

We recently watched *Blackfish*, a fascinating documentary on killer whales, and it spoke to us so powerfully. The whales were taken out of the wild and into captivity and the effect on their lives was extreme. These whales normally swim hundreds of miles a day, and yet they were being taken out of the open water into small tanks that seriously limited their movement. In the wild, they were living for up to seventy-five years, and in captivity, their life span became a maximum of just thirty-five years. When the whales were free, their fins were pointing up and they were healthy and liberated, but in captivity, their fins were bent over and their temperament affected. Having been peaceful creatures, they were becoming violent with one another and with human trainers. One of the whales had ended up attacking a trainer and killing her. In contrast, there is no record of any killer whale attacking a human in the wild, ever.

What struck us the most was that these mammals were living in an environment that was killing them, robbing them of life, and causing their behaviour to change. It got us thinking that we are not called to live in captivity; we are designed for freedom. Are we in any way being taken out of our natural habitat, moved into confined spaces, and limited from swimming the miles we were designed to cover? What is our culture moulding us into? We have talked about being asleep. Is our culture also forcing us into cages of fear and small confined spaces of busyness, sucking us of life in all its fullness? Our creator designed us to soar, to experience life in all its fullness, to be filled with living water because the author of life has poured it into us. We do not want to conform to the pattern of this world but be transformed by the power of God and his Spirit breathing life into us so we can demonstrate a new way to truly live.

We read an article with extracts from a documentary called *Sheep Among Wolves* that talked about an Iranian couple who had gone to the USA. After just a couple of months, the wife had really started to struggle and wanted to move back to Iran, telling her husband, 'There is a satanic lullaby here. All the Christians are sleepy and I'm feeling sleepy.' In the article the alarming nature of her conclusion is written about: 'This story was disturbing because that woman was discerning a threat to her faith that was far greater than the kind of persecution that happens in Iran. She saw that spiritual sleepiness is a greater threat to her faith than persecution.'[1]

The problem is that we need to make space for saints to be real about the fight that they are in, and we need to love one another in a way that enables us to be vulnerable. Remember *Sleeping Beauty*: Jesus didn't just come for the mighty prince riding on his stallion with his mighty sword in hand. He also came for the son and daughter surrounded by, and consumed by, bushes of pain and suffering, trying to beat their way through to freedom.

Church cannot be a place where we dress up, act a part, and convince the congregation that 'everything is all right with me.' The British act of 'keeping up appearances' has to die; the reserve that guards the mess has to fall. Christy Wimber puts it this way: 'The messier the church is the more we know we're doing exactly what we are called to do. We are not to enshrine our sainthood as if people in pain don't exist; we must become what is missing, not only for others but also for ourselves.'[2]

It's getting messy in the UK, and we need to create a space where people are safe to come and share their mess. If we don't open up our hearts and lives to each other in repentance, honesty, forgiveness, and willing restoration, then how can we expect the lost to truly meet the king of the world? Sometimes we think no one is looking, but they are, and they are hungry for an authentic Christianity that can truly transform their life.

It has often been said that the Welsh Revivalists would get in a circle and pray like their whole life depended on it, declaring 'Start with the sinner in the circle.' Throughout history, revivals are noted for being filled with deep confession, public emotion, and realization of the desperate need to be saved.

We have begun to pray at church in a new way. To repent regularly, corporately. To share communion and to cry out to God that he would send a new wave of his Holy Spirit, starting with us. The Iranian church appeared to be so broken, so weak, and yet was so united, so strong. They were infectious because they were on fire with the spirit of the Living God. The fire surrounded them and filled each and every one of them because they knew they were living sacrifices, broken on the altar of the king, longing for him to move in power.

We believe that the army the Lord rising in the west needs to look to the example of the army in the east. Take China for example: 'it has been estimated that 10,000 people per day become Christ followers, and even by conservative estimates, Christianity has grown by 4,300 percent in 50 years. By 2030, China will have more Christians living in it than any other nation on earth.'[3] As the kingdom forces rise and advance, they send international echoes from the Acts church; they point us to Jesus and to a church unleashed.

Prison sentences and persecution were not just a common theme in Acts—they are, right now, a reality for our brothers and sisters. Now knowing a few who have suffered for Christ, we read Acts with new lenses—it feels more real than it ever has before because we can picture our friends right in the midst of these pages.

In Acts 16, Paul and Silas have been stripped and beaten, then imprisoned. They are in the inner cell with their feet fastened in stocks. Think back to Peter in Acts 12 and Peter and John in Acts 4—this is not the first time we hear prison mentioned. Now Paul and Silas are far from being 'unleashed' in this moment. They are completely and utterly 'leashed'—in darkness, naked, sores all over their bodies, and it could be their final night alive. We think that in this moment we would be crying in pain, weeping with sadness, hoping with everything in us that an angel would come as it did for Peter in Acts 12, or for the apostles in Acts 5:19, and lead them out. However, that is not the reality.

So, obviously, the most natural thing to do in this moment is to start singing hymns to God and praying? (Acts 16:25). We cannot believe that the apostles in this place of agony begin to worship Jesus. One commentator notes: 'The one thing you can never take away from a Christian is God and the presence of Jesus Christ. 'With God there is freedom even in a prison and even at midnight there is light.'[4]

In this place of prayer and worship we then witness the most incredible breakthrough: an earthquake that shakes the foundations of the prison, opens the doors, and the chains come loose! (16:26-27). What is really important here is that Paul and Silas are not worshipping *after* that release but *before* it. They are singing to Jesus in the pain and darkness. Sometimes things can get extremely painful and difficult just before we see mighty breakthroughs.

God is looking for a church that will pray, that will worship him no matter what state their life is in, and no matter how bleak the outcome looks. The Spirit of God takes up his home in our hearts to empower us to worship in the darkness. To be a church unleashed requires learning to worship no matter how we feel, what is happening, or what could happen. We find this so challenging.

Our Iranian friend talks about being at home with her parents when the police came to take her sister away to prison. She begged them not to cuff her and take her. Her sister was being taken because of how she had been sharing her faith in Jesus with people and handing out Bibles. As the door closed and her sister was suddenly gone, our friend fell to the floor in floods of tears—her whole world torn apart in a matter of moments. Instead of her parents joining her on their knees to weep, something bizarre happened. Her mum took her by the hand and said, 'Do not cry daughter. We must worship the Lord.' Drawing herself slowly to her feet, legs wobbling and eyes misty, she began to worship Jesus. As they worshipped and prayed together, faith rose and courage returned. A couple of hours later the police returned for the other daughter.

We were so deeply moved hearing this story, and at first we wanted to argue it. Why not let her be to cry? Why worship in such a place of horror? And yet, bit by bit, we realised something: the enemy wants us to give up, to lie down and die, to steal our hope and sense of purpose. But the Lord wants us to keep advancing and trusting him no matter what.

Check out these words in Isaiah—there is a clear call for us to take responsibility, to choose not to let our circumstances make us lie down: 'Awake, Awake, O Zion, clothe *yourself* with strength. Put on *your* garments of splendour, O Jerusalem the Holy City. The circumcised and defiled will not enter you again. Shake off *your* dust; *rise up*, sit enthroned, O Jerusalem. Free *yourself* from the chains on your neck, O captive daughter of Zion' (Isaiah 52:1-2). Sometimes there is a mighty move of God in our circumstances, but other times, we have to make deliberate choices to keep moving forward in faith. We decide that we are not going to be defeated by our situation and so we choose to worship instead of weep, declare truth instead of lie down in a bed of lies, and wake up to the greatness of our God rather than letting the oppressor pin us to a perspective of darkness.

The army that the Lord is raising is a word and spirit army who set their faces like flint to walk into the darkness. Setting our faces like flint to advance involves sheer, utter determination. We definitely have moments where determination is severely lacking, however, this is where the Spirit comes to us. This is the moment to say, 'We can't, God, but you can. Please fill us with your strength to fight again; please enable us to stand.' There have to be ways we can still advance in the darkness. Joel 3:9-10 says, 'Proclaim this among the nations: Prepare for war! Rouse the warriors! Let all the fighting men draw near and attack. Beat your ploughshares into swords and your pruning hooks into spears. Let the weakling say, "I am strong!", We rouse and awaken through worship, prayer, adoration, and declaration, and as we do it, something shifts in us: strength rises, the Spirit empowers, and we are reminded that the Lord Almighty has the victory.

As we begin to arise and stand in the battle, we are transformed. 'Great faith is the product of great fights. Great testimonies are the outcome of great tests. Great triumphs can only come out of great trials. Every stumbling block must become a stepping stone and every opposition must become an opportunity.'[5] Lord, grant us this perspective, that we can accept those words from James: 'Consider it pure joy, my brothers, whenever you face trials of many kinds, because you know that the testing of your faith develops persever-ance. Perseverance must finish its work so that you may be mature and complete not lacking anything' (James 1:2-4).

In the UK Too

An unleashed church can force the hospitality industry to hire peo-ple differently, turning dodgy temp jobs into careers. It can amplify the simplest neighbourly acts, like saying hello, into a movement combatting loneliness. And it will definitely use food (growing, cooking, eating, shopping) to make the richest kingdom parties ac-cessible and delightful to the most excluded people in the city.

All of these things are afoot at One Church Brighton, where a Baptist congregation is flourishing into a Sussex-wide community of farmers and farmers, market shoppers, baristas and barkeeps, single mothers, and (recovering) street sleepers. In any given month, more than 1,000 people fill the community throughout its various expres-sions: inside a shared, 16th-century farmhouse; on council estates; in coffee shops; under vegetable polytunnels; and in church on Sun-day morning.

Driving this expression of church is a growing awareness of those left behind. For example, one in three children in parts of Brighton & Hove lives in poverty. For thirteen weeks each year, when schools are not in session, the loss of a free school meal means lunch can disap-pear for thousands of families. Food poverty stunts a child's ability to learn in school, isolates families, and sets up a cascade of ill effects that ripple through the National Health Service, the housing system, the job centre, and beyond. The political and social case for better food service couldn't be stronger, at a time when the UK wastes more than half of all the food produced.

In response, the project Chomp is feeding families—often using surplus ingredients—while offering social support. Thousands of meals provided in nine Brighton locations go some of the way, but the social connections can go even further, helping lonely mothers become ecstatic community members. Some of these urban families landed recently on the rural One Church project called Rock Farm to taste the locally grown vegetables, experience the nourishment that comes from nature connection, and immerse themselves in an extraordinarily diverse crowd. Rock Farm produces local produce while offering therapeutic horticulture to a diverse group of marginalised people, and Chomp families were the latest group to enjoy the benefits of being embedded together in nature.

Never before, said one grandfather, had such a day out been possible for his family. The acres of safe space, the healthy food, the sense of belonging to a community, and the bottomless cups of specialty coffee—it simply doesn't happen under normal circumstances.

The coffee was produced by Pro Baristas, another One Church project, connecting unemployed people with the exploding market for coffee jobs. To make these careers satisfying, it becomes necessary to change the way businesses hire, lowering staff turnover costs, and building reliable jobs for the people who need them most. Through industry events and consulting relationships, Pro Baristas has managed to alter the employment landscape in coffee, putting hundreds into work while hundreds more have found a scintillating way to stretch themselves, join a supportive group, and hatch plans for the future.

Like the early church followers huddled in houses, this sort of flourishing is not without struggle and instability. Indeed, perhaps we mostly live in that space, learning to expect that seeds will sprout in marginal scrub. Along these margins, we find the natural members of an energized church, and, like most of us, they tend to flourish when they discover a church-run farmers' market on their doorstep, or a shared housing scheme in the West Sussex countryside open to people with very different stories to share.

These are actions aimed at both struggling individuals and structural injustices in a time of devastating government cutbacks and a swell of inequality. 'There comes a point,' Desmond Tutu said, 'where we need to stop just pulling people out of the river. We need to go up-stream and find out why they're falling in.' To 'unleash' the church means more than an outbreak of niceness. It leads instead to sys-temic change—a materialization of God's kingdom, full of equality and justice, for the entire community.

Yes, but How?

For you:

If you are in a difficult place and you feel in darkness or in chains:

Isaiah 51:22 *'This is what the Sovereign Lord says, your God who defends his people:*
See I have taken out of your hand the cup that made you stagger; from that cup, the goblet of my wrath, you will never drink again. I will put it into the hands of your tormentors, who said to you, "fall prostrate that we may walk over you" and you made your back like the ground, like a street to be walked over.'

Call upon the Lord who saves you, who calls you to arise and sit enthroned.
Call on him and ask him to take away the cup that makes you personally stagger.
Perhaps your cup is one of the following: fear, power, lust, control, low self-image, feeling stuck, lack of faith, or too much food, drink, internet, etc. the things that keep you in chains.
As you think about your cup of struggle, ask the Lord to put it/them back into the hands of your tormentors.
Declare that he the only one who can do that.
Ask the Lord to strengthen you with his mighty power so that you will not lie down and be walked over again.

For your group:

Godreports.com's 'Sheep among Wolves' article cites, 'If freedom is such a great thing for the Kingdom, then why are Europe and America in the state they are in?'

1 What do you think about this?
2 Is freedom always a good thing?

3 Do you think we have to face persecution to get serious about, and focussed on, Jesus?

4 Can we see a major move of God in the UK without the backdrop of oppression and persecution?

Further reading:

M. Bradley, *Too Many to Jail* (Oxford: Monarch Books, 2014)

Brother Yun, *The Heavenly Man* (Oxford: Monarch Books, 2002)

16

Making a Difference

'Remember, each one of us has the power to change the world.'
Yoko Ono

The Austrian neurologist, psychiatrist, and Holocaust survivor, Viktor Frankl, devoted his life to studying, understanding, and promoting purpose. His famous book, *Man's Search for Meaning*, tells the story of how he survived the Holocaust by finding personal meaning in the experience, which gave him the will to live through it. He argues that in the absence of meaning, people fill the resultant void with hedonistic pleasures, power, materialism, hatred, boredom, or neurotic obsessions and compulsion.[1] Right now in our nation there is certainly an absence of meaning for many, and this is leading to all manner of difficulty as many seek to fill this void with unsatisfactory things. Some of these other things bring an instant buzz or sense of pleasure, but like fast food, the impact is only short-lived and the long-term damage to our health is very much present.

The French mathematician and Christian philosopher Blaise Pascal took this argument further when he said that the search was not just for meaning but for God: 'There is a God-shaped vacuum in the heart of every man which cannot be filled by any created thing, but only by God, the Creator, made known through Jesus.' Many are searching for contentment and happiness elsewhere, but this can only be met in Jesus. The challenge is how we, as the church, support and help people whilst they are struggling so much with many of the challenges they are facing or with the inevitable results of filling a god-shaped hole with something other than God.

Many of these issues and challenges are being felt most acutely in younger generations. Young people seem under more pressure than ever, and the fact that our society is more broken than previously only exacerbates this reality. Research from the Prince's Trust has found that young people's happiness across every single area of their lives has never been lower.[2] What's so striking here is that it's not just in one area of their lives that things are hard. With the pressure to perform within our education system, it would be understandable if the pressure to succeed here was too much, but this research shows that young people are struggling in every context.

The famous atheist Stephen Fry said when asked about why so many children and young people are so unhappy: 'We can say, but look, they've got everything—they've got iPhones, they've got this, they've got that. Clearly, we know that can't be enough. There is something missing.'[3] Fry's diagnosis of the problem is spot on, though as an atheist he would certainly struggle to prescribe the solution. He argues this based on the incredible level of distraction it brings about.[4] Our current culture is so rapid, pressurized, unfulfilled, and often empty. We are part of this culture, but that does not mean that for one minute we have to simply be part of it, accepting all of the cultural norms associated too. The theologian Dan Strange argues in his book, *Plugged In*, that though what technology we consume will have an impact on us, we don't have to simply become a result of all that it chooses to message as normal. He argues that 'it's possible to consume culture without either being bewitched by it—buying into everything it tells us—or bewildered by it.'[5] We are called to be part of the culture we find ourselves in, but not to be overwhelmingly subsumed into it. We are salt and light and as such need to influence and shape the culture, not simply be passive magnolia wallpaper on the world's agenda.

Another Way?

At one of the summer conferences, our friend discovered a room full of young people worshipping. It was late at night, all the 'regular' meetings were over, and yet there they were, 'out of hours,' a large number of teenagers pressing in to meet with God. If we think back to being younger, we would have been up at that hour too but most definitely not in prayer and worship—rather round the campfire with drinks in hand. Something deeply struck us when we heard this. Young people may have it all, and yet they are so empty and lost—they are driven to the feet of Jesus out of a total desperation for him. They are poor in spirit and hungry for something that can satisfy, so they are turning to Christ. We wonder whether the weakness and brokenness in the younger generation will actually be the catalyst for a mighty move of God in the nation. Perhaps the unleashing of the church will arise from the young as they seek in a way that the older generations have not found 'time' to? We feel led to turn our attention to the youth and not just pray for them, but watch how they are beginning to pray.

We have felt God driving home to us the reality that we must not limit his children based on their age, or experience, or on their gender, or social class. If he is indeed raising up the young, then we need to look for, and recognise, the hand of God on their lives and release them to exercise the call that is growing on and through them. We have also felt challenged as part of the 'older' church to role model a way of 'doing' church that might look different: more accessible, open, flexible, and embracing. Not a church that will immediately push them into years of training, tell them to wait until they are older, or are perceived as 'sorted'. It makes us ask, how can we create stepping-stones for the young that can enable them to fully follow Jesus, and for us not to stand in their way when they need to lead?

We also don't need to be Christian superheroes. Let's start facing up to the reality that we all struggle, we all have moments of doubt and challenge. We're sure that no one has gone through life not feeling like they are engaging in 'imposter syndrome.' Our experience has been that the weaker we are, the more the Lord uses us. Certainly when we've been vulnerable about our challenges over the years (such as our many struggles having children), it's out of our weakness and honesty that the Lord has moved powerfully. For Gavin, being told by doctors that he probably couldn't have children, has transformed his ministry. Mercifully, we have had two kids, but from the day of those fertility results, he has ministered out of brokenness and not a previous self-confidence that could have tipped over into arrogance. Rick Warren writes that 'If you want God to bless you and use you greatly, you must be willing to walk with a limp the rest of your life, because God uses weak people.'[6] He must use people like this if his power is made perfect in weakness.

What About the Church?

This extract from a letter that Dr. Martin Luther King Jr. wrote is so challenging. Dubbed 'the Letter from Birmingham Jail,' it's an open letter written on April 16, 1963, from his prison cell. It defends the strategy of nonviolent resistance to racism whilst also drawing clear attention to the state of the church:

> There was a time when the church was very powerful—in the time when the early Christians rejoiced at being deemed worthy to suffer for what they believed. In those days the church was not merely a thermometer that recorded the ideas and principles of popular opinion; it was a thermostat that transformed the mores of society. Wherever the early Christians entered a town the power structure got disturbed and immediately sought to convict them for being 'disturbers of the peace' and 'outside agitators.' But they went on with the conviction that they were 'a colony of heaven' and had to obey God rather than man.

Small in number, they were big in commitment. They were too God-intoxicated to be 'astronomically intimidated.' By their effort and example they brought an end to such ancient evils as infanticide and gladiatorial contests. Things are different now. So often the contemporary church is a weak, ineffectual voice with an uncertain sound.[7]

Dr. Martin Luther King Jr. was trying to provoke the church into action and draw clear attention to the fact that we were getting it wrong in so many ways. He was right, but we also have a danger of looking at all of the New Testament church through rose-tinted spectacles as the following story shows.

A young man named Mark had just become a Christian, so he was looking for a good local church to attend. One Sunday he went along to the church that was situated closest to him, but he was shocked by what he discovered was taking place. It wasn't just the savage gossip that he overheard before the service began—there were plenty of other things going on that he hadn't expected to find. There was the sermon that denied the resurrection of Christ. Then the quarrelling that broke out during Holy Communion, and the group of people who got up and walked out during the prayer time.

After the service, someone took the time to fill Mark in on all the latest gossip about others in the church. He explained how two members of the congregation were taking legal action against each other. He exposed the fact that one individual was carrying on an affair with his stepmother. He also elaborated on the presence of internal strife and party rivalry, and on the way in which the church looked highly likely to undergo a four-way split. In the light of this disconcerting visit, Mark returned home and started to have serious second thoughts about his newfound faith.

Mark's case study does raise some serious pastoral problems for us. It creates questions that are not easy to answer. Is Mark's an isolated experience? Are many churches that vulnerable to a probing, though sympathetic, examination? Perhaps the advice that would most readily be given to Mark might focus on his need to look elsewhere and try to find a different church, to concentrate on seeking out a church more closely modelled on New Testament lines. That advice sounds fine in theory; the only problem is that the church Mark went to was not only patterned on the New Testament ideal of church, it was a New Testament church. For Mark was a citizen of the first century, and his local church was the church at Corinth.'[8]

Our churches today may not have the same difficulties, but they can be just as ostracizing to the people of the twenty-first century as the church in Corinth was to Mark all those centuries ago. No period of time is perfect, so we choose to live in our day, act accordingly, and do all we can to reach our generation for Jesus.

Always Hopeful of Impact

Yes, the church is not perfect, but under the authority of Jesus there is so much difference it can make. Another key factor is strong leadership. For fourteen years we lived in Halesowen in the West Midlands. Halesowen is an interesting place of about 60,000 people that sits on the very end of the Black Country or the very edge of Birmingham, depending on who you ask. It is also one of the largest places in the UK to be based right on a motorway junction and not be singed from it. Whilst there, we got to know one of the greatest church leaders we've ever met, Leon Evans. Here he tells a little of his story in being *unleashed* to reach more people.

We were stuck . . . we wanted to reach more people, to impact more lives and we were trying hard. We felt the best way to do that was build a bigger building, so we raised money and bought adjacent land but we were still stuck. Then in August 2015, it seemed to get worse as a fire destroyed our auditorium. What happened next was amazing, the church dug deep, the community came to help and soon we were back in business, only this time something deeper and more far reaching was beginning to stir.

We wanted to reach more people but what if building a bigger building wasn't the only way to do it? What if we planted some other expressions of who we were in communities close by that didn't have an expression of church quite like us? What if we went multisite, one church in many locations? So we began to pray for a village nearby called Hagley; seen by many as a growing community. Lots of people wanted to live there for the schools and the commute into Birmingham.

So we began the process of doing our research, talking to other multisite churches, casting vision to the church in Halesowen. Then on Easter Sunday 2017, a group of 30 people began Lifecentral Hagley meeting in a high school. We've just celebrated 2 years and are seeing new people every week many of whom are unchurched or dechurched! We've had baptisms and incredible stories of God at work in people's lives.

Now we are establishing community connection points in the village such as a pre-school club, a youth club and running Alpha in one of the pubs. We have a saying we try to live by, "don't let a crowd form in your community that you are not a part of!" So we look for what's happening and then serve and get involved. It's amazing what God does when we step out.

As if that wasn't exciting enough, at the end of 2017, we were approached by another church close to us but in a very different area than Hagley. The Brickhouse Elim church has been in existence since the 1960s on a disadvantaged estate, but the church was now just a few older people. They graciously asked if we would take them on, and they laid down all leadership and handed us the building. Even though we didn't feel ready, we felt God's leading and so on Easter Sunday 2018, we began to repurpose that church as Lifecentral Rowley.

That faithful handful of older Christians are still with us, but have now been joined by many others; families have joined, people have become Christians, and life is bursting out not only in the church but on the estate. The prayers of these faithful believers are starting to be answered!

For us our unleashing was a natural fire that resulted in a spiritual fire, and now two new communities are beginning to see new spiritual life. We believe there's much more to come!

We know Halesowen so well and so find Leon's story all the more encouraging. We need to be innovating, planting in new communities, dreaming for our locations, and being a people of hope. In a world that can feel so desolate and hopeless, we need to be the great bringers of hope because we know Jesus. It was the Greek philosopher Aristotle who said that 'hope is a waking dream.' Let's keep living it.

Yes, but How?

For you:

1 What is holding you back from stepping into all the Lord has for you?
2 What might you need to break free from or leave behind?
3 Ask the Lord for things to be different moving forward.

For your group:

1 How can our churches be places where people can find freedom?
2 What might we need to change in what we are doing to help those struggling?
3 Are we releasing enough younger leaders?
4 What needs to change to help younger generations thrive?
5 How can we all be less distracted by technology?

A couple of ministries wanting to help us break free:

Kintsugi Hope

Patrick and Diane Regan are pioneering a great new ministry called Kintsugi Hope. They offer all kinds of ways to help people through the church. Kintsugi Hope groups work in communities through the local church with an attitude of humility—not to judge, fix, or rescue, but to come alongside and love one another. We are all broken in some ways, and we can all learn from each other. More info here: https://www.kintsugihope.com

Mind and Soul

Mind and Soul believe in a God who loves us and cares about our emotional and mental health. Our faith and emotions are often kept separate. Mental health is rarely discussed in churches, and Christian spirituality is seen as having little to offer the world of psychology. They want to bridge that gap. Their website is: https://www.mindandsoulfoundation.org.

Further Reading:

P. Regan, *Honesty over Silence: It's OK not to be OK* (Farnham: CWR, 2018)

W. Van Der Hart, R. Waller, *The Power of Belonging* (Colorado: David C Cook, 2019)

Conclusion

'Everyone has a part to play. We have the power. You can do it.'
Maxine Waters

As we pen these last words we find ourselves in a new season. It's true that we don't seem to be able to write a book without beginning to journey it. Well, at least you can know that this narrative is as authentic as we could hope. Gavin is now the CEO of the Evangelical Alliance seeking to unite the church to reach the lost. In a world of unease and political tensions, we stand on hope, believing that for such a time as this, the Lord is going to do more than we could ever ask or imagine according to his power that's at work within us all (Ephesians 3:20-21). We can allow the enemy to highlight all the challenges that lie ahead (which is sometimes easy to do) or we can together, across the church, rise up with hope, fixing our eyes on Jesus, remembering he has the victory.

Recently I, Anne, was awake very early in the morning and believe the Lord was calling me to look up 'sleeping' in his Word. If you haven't done it, it is fascinating. What appeared to jump out was the reality that Jonah ran away from God's call to go to Nineveh. In his disobedience he boarded a boat, a storm blew up, and he lay in a deep sleep below deck (1:5). He was in a deep sleep in the midst of a mighty storm. He ran away from God, he tried to hide, and he became oblivious to the state of things around him. I found myself praying that the Lord would keep me from disobedience, and help us, as the church, not to run away in fear but face the wave that is coming. We do not want to sleep through a move of the mighty one.

In Judges, Delilah causes Samson to fall asleep; she deceives him and cuts off his hair while he is sleeping (16:19). Samson loses all power during that sleep; he loses what the Lord has given him because of the power of seduction. We have an enemy who is on the prowl and seeking to put us to sleep or keep us asleep so that we lose sight of our gifts and the power somehow melts away.

The disciples were sleeping right before Jesus was arrested (Matthew 26:40-46). A pivotal moment in history, a time when we wish we had been alive and in prayer. A key time to be watchful, to be awake, and yet the disciples cannot stay awake. There is so much that the Lord wants to open our spiritual eyes to, so much he doesn't want us to miss at this key time in history. We are praying for ourselves, and for the church, that we will not sleepwalk our way to death and miss what the Lord might do by his Holy Spirit.

Zechariah 4:1-2 says 'Then the angel woke me up like someone awakened from a deep sleep. He asked me, "What do you see?"' Lord, let us be woken from our spiritual slumber, let us hear the sound of the trumpet call, and let us see what you want us to see. Ephesians 5:14: 'Wake up Oh sleeper and rise from the dead and Christ will shine on you!' Lord, please shine on us, please fill us with the power of your Spirit, overflow us with the love of God and a love for your people.

As we conclude, we pray that these words have helped you in some small way to think about your church, our church, his people, and have equipped you with greater power and discernment to live out all that he has called us to in the days to come.

The book of Acts is itself an unfinished work. We have loved digging into it and have covered the beginnings of the church in Acts 1-12. Moving further on, Acts 13-28 covers the development of the church seen in the Pauline case study. We are now given the responsibility of writing the final chapter, Acts 29. That's why the book of Acts lacks a comfortable conclusion. It still is not finished. The church, ever since, has been writing Acts 29, which remains to be concluded and continues until he returns.

Let's make sure we play our part in our day. Go for it!

Final Thought

Sometimes the words of an old song can sum up just where we sense
the Spirit is drawing the church towards. Why not take a moment as
you finish this book to read these words and pray as you feel led that
the Lord would indeed raise up an army, that the church of Jesus
Christ in the UK to be truly unleashed and to see the nations transformed by his power and love.

'I Hear the Sound of Rustling' by Ronnie Wilson

I hear the sound of rustling in the leaves of the trees
The Spirit of the Lord has come down on the earth
The church that seemed in slumber has now risen from its knees
And dry bones are responding with the fruits of new birth
Oh, this is now a time for declaration
The word will go to all men everywhere
The church is here for healing of the nations
Behold the day of Jesus drawing near

My tongue will be the pen of a ready writer
And what the Father gives to me I'll sing
I only want to be His breath
I only want to glorify the King

And all around the world the body waits expectantly
The promise of the Father is now ready to fall
The watchmen on the tower all exhort us to prepare
And the church responds-a people who will answer the call
And this is not a phase which is passing
It's the start of an age that is to come
And where is the wise man and the scoffer?
Before the face of Jesus they are dumb

A body now prepared by God and ready for war
The prompting of the Spirit is our word of command
We rise, a mighty army, at the bidding of the Lord
The devils see and fear, for their time is at hand
And children of the Lord hear our commission
That we should love and serve our God as one
The Spirit won't be hindered by division
In the perfect work that Jesus has begun*

---

* Extract taken from the song 'I Hear the Sound of Rustling' by Ronnie Wilson.
Copyright © 1979 Thankyou Music

Notes

Introduction

1 G. Calver, S. Whiting, *Lazy, Anti-social & Selfish?* (Oxford: Monarch Books, 2009), .30.

2 W. Wiersbe, *The Bible Exposition Commentary* (Wheaton: Victor Books, 1996, John 1:35)

3 B. Milne, *The Message of John* (Leicester: IVP, 1993) .58

4 F. Chan, *Crazy Love* (Colorado: David C Cook, 2008) .22

5 D. Bonhoeffer, *The Cost of Discipleship* (London: SCM Press, 1959) .104

6 R.T. Kendall, C. Carrin, J. Taylor, *Word Spirit Power* (Bloomington: Chosen Books, 2012) .78

7 P. Moore, *Straight to the Heart of Acts* (Oxford: Monarch Books, 2010) .76

8 M. Muggeridge, *Another King* (Edinburgh: St. Andrew Press, 1968) .47

9 J. Trousdale, G. Sunshine, *The Kingdom Unleashed* (Murfreesboro: DMM Library, 2018) .4

1 The Holy Spirit Comes

1 J. Wimber, *Power Evangelism* (London: Hodder & Stoughton, 2013) .61

2 T. Wright, *Acts for Everyone* (London: SPCK, 2012) .3

3 T. Wright, *Acts for Everyone* (London: SPCK, 2012) .4

4 *The NIV Zondervan Study Bible*, (London: Hodder & Stoughton, 2017, paraphrased) .2207-2208

5 J. Stott, *The Message of Acts* (Leicester: IVP, 1990) .60

6 J. Cymbala, *Fresh Wind, Fresh Fire* (Grand Rapids. Zondervan 2018). 18

7   A. Fernando, *The NIV Application Commentary: Acts* (Grand Rapids: Zondervan, 1998) .86

8   W. Neil, *The Acts of the Apostles* (Grand Rapids: Eerdmans, 1986) .71

9   J. Stott, *The Message of Acts* (Leicester: IVP 1990) .62

10 J. Boice, *Acts 'An Expositional Commentary,'* (Grand Rapids: Baker Books, 2007) .39

11 F.F. Bruce, *The Book of Acts* (London: Marshall, Morgan & Scott, Ltd., 1968) .54

12 P. Moore, *Straight to the heart of Acts* (Oxford: Lion Hudson, 2010) .33

13 D. Pytches, *Come, Holy Spirit* (London: Hodder & Stoughton, 1985) .140

14 C. Calver, *The Holy Spirit* (Milton Keynes: Scripture Union, 2001) .42

15 M. Tanner, *The Introvert Charismatic* (Oxford: Monarch Books, 2015) .14

16 I. Howard Marshall, *Acts* (Leicester: IVP, 1980) .60-61

2 Time for Act 2

1   P. Moore, *Straight to the Heart of Acts* (Oxford: Lion Hudson, 2010) .29

2   F. Chan, *Letters to the Church* (Colorado: David C Cook, 2018) .39

3   R. Parsons, *What they didn't teach me in Sunday School* (London: Hodder & Stoughton, 1998) .22

4   M. Green, *The Message of Matthew* (Leicester: IVP, 2000) .180

5   W. Wiersbe, *The Bible Exposition Commentary* (Colorado Springs: Chariot Victor Publishing, 2003) .59

6   E.M. Blaiklock, *Acts* (Leicester: IVP, 1959) .60

7   T. Wright, *Acts for Everyone* (London: SPCK 2008) .32

8   A. Scott, *Scattered Servants* (Colorado Springs: David C. Cook, 2018) .23

9   F. Chan, *Letters to the Church* (Colorado: David C Cook, 2018) .27

3 Walking On Water

1 M. Macdonald, *Set Me On Fire* (Oxford: Monarch Books, 2015) .7

2 Directed by Michael Apted, 2007

3 http://edition.cnn.com/2008/WORLD/africa/06/24/mandela. quotes/

4 J. E. Smith, *The Books of History* (Joplin: College Press Publishing Company, 1995) .189

5 https://www.telegraph.co.uk/family/relationships/ cant-tell-wife-go-church-pretend-go-cycling-instead/

6 If you are interested in exploring Urban Mission, please visit joineden.org for more information.

7 W. Kaiser, *The Preacher's Commentary Series, Volume 23* (Nashville: Thomas Nelson Publishers, 1992) .339

8 https://www.premierchristianity.com/Past-Issues/2017/April-2017 /RT-Kendall-How-the-church-fell-asleep-and-why-it-needs-to- wake-up

4 Independent Living

1 B. Milne, *The Message of John* (Leicester: IVP, 1993) .316

2 F. Chan, *Letters to the Church* (Colorado: David C Cook, 2018) .86

3 A. Fernando, K. Lee-Thorp, *Acts 'The Message of Jesus in Action'* (Grand Rapids: Zondervan, 2010) .44

4 L. Alexander, *Acts* (Oxford: BRF, 2006) .46

5 J. Stott, *The Message of Acts* (Leicester: IVP, 1990) .81

6 I. Howard Marshall, *Acts* (Leicester: IVP, 1980) .83

7 W. Neil, *The Acts of the Apostles* (Grand Rapids: Eerdmans, 1986) .82

8 T. Wright, *Acts for Everyone* (London: SPCK, 2012) .45

9 J. Stott, *The Message of Acts* (Leicester: IVP, 1990) .82, 84, 86

10 P. Moore, *Straight to the heart of Acts* (Oxford: Lion Hudson, 2010) .67-68

11 M. Backholer, *Revival Fire 150 years of Revivals* (ByFaith media, 2017) .6-7

5 Living as One

1 S. Clifford, *One* (Oxford: Monarch Books, 2017) .112

2 For more do visit https://www.eauk.org/what-we-do/networks
/one-people-commission

3 T. Wright, *John for Everyone* (London: SPCK, 2002) .92

4 M. Duncan, *One for All: The Foundations* (Oxford: Monarch
Books, 2017) .84

5 I. Randall, D. Hilborn, *One Body in Christ: The History &
Significance of the Evangelical Alliance* (Carlisle: Paternoster Press,
2001) .37

6 R.V.G. Tasker, *John* (Leicester: IVP, 1999) .191

7 B. Milne, *The Message of John* (Leicester: IVP, 1993) .240-242

8 R. Sutton (editor), *A Gathering Momentum* (Watford: Instant
Apostle, 2017) .223-224

9 *21ˢᵗ Century Evangelicals* (London: Evangelical Alliance, 2011)

10 G. Calver, *Disappointed with Jesus?* (Oxford: Monarch Books,
2010) .8

11 *Talking Jesus: Perceptions of Jesus, Christians and Evangelism in
England* (Research from the Barna Group on behalf of the Church
of England, Evangelical Alliance and Hope, 2015) .38

12 For more information on these clubs check out www.resources.yfc
.co.uk

13 F. Chan, *Letters to the Church* (Colorado: David C Cook, 2018) .15

14 A. Hirsch, *5 Q's* (100 movements, 2017) .13

6 Playing Your Part

1 M. Greene, *Fruitfulness on the Frontline* (Nottingham: IVP, 2014)

2 M. Wilcock, *The Message of Luke* (Leicester: IVP, 1979) .182

3 https://starfishproject.com/the-parable/

4 T. Wright, *Acts for Everyone* (London: SPCK 2008) .101

5 https://factsandtrends.
net/2019/06/11/7-surprising-trends-in-global-christianity-in-2019/

7 Ministering Together

1 Directed by Peter Jackson, 2001

2 F. Chan, *Letters to the Church* (Colorado: David C Cook, 2018) .90

3 J. Boice, *Acts 'An Expositional commentary,'* (Grand Rapids: Baker Books, 2007) .203

4 P. Harcourt, R. Turner, *Greater Things 'The Story of New Wine So Far'* (London: SPCK, 2019) .45

5 C. Groeschel, HTB Leadership Conference, Royal Albert Hall. 2019

6 C. Groeschel, HTB Leaders Conference. Royal Albert Hall, 2019

8 Empowered to Share

1 S. Bevans, R. Schroeder, *Prophetic Dialogue* (Maryknoll: Orbis Books, 2009) .1

2 I.H. Marshall, *Acts* (Leicester: IVP, 1980) .114

3 J. Stott, *The Message of Acts* (Leicester: IVP, 1990) .112

4 R. C. Sproul, *The Holiness of God* (Carol Stream: Tyndall House, 2000) .68

5 W. Neil, *The Acts of the Apostles* (Grand Rapids: Eerdmans, 1986) .96

6 J. Stott, *The Message of Acts* (Leicester: IVP, 1990) .114

7 D. Field, *James* (Leicester: Crossways Books, 1998) .24

8 T. Wright, *Acts for Everyone* (London: SPCK, 2008) .88

9 L. Newbigin, *'Cross-Currents in Ecumenical and Evangelical Understandings of Mission'* (*International Bulletin of Missionary Research, 1982)* .146

10 *The Guardian Newspaper,* 30th January 2019

11 M. Green, *The Message of Matthew* (Leicester: IVP, 2000) .321

12 M. Green, *The Message of Matthew* (Leicester: IVP, 2000) .323

13 For more information on Advance do visit www.advance2020.org

9 Signs of the Times

1 J. M. Comer, *The Ruthless Elimination of Hurry* (Colorado Springs: Waterbrook Press, 2019).

2 P. Dixon, *The Future of (Almost) Everything* (London: Profile Books Ltd., 2019) .17

3 www.statisticbrain.com/attention-span-statistics/

4 https://www.nytimes.com/2019/01/25/opinion/sunday/steve-jobs -never-wanted-us-to-use-our-iphones-like-this.html

5 This Cultural Moment podcast, series 1, episode 3

6 https://www.vanityfair.com/news/2018/07 /the-man-who-created-the-world-wide-web-has-some-regrets

7 https://www.theguardian.com/technology/2017/oct/05 /smartphone-addiction-silicon-valley-dystopia

8 A. Flintoff, *Do You Know What?* (London: Blink Publishing, 2018) .293

9 Should we dislike the 'Like' button? https://www.bbc.co.uk/news /business-48364817

10 J.K.A. Smith, *How (Not) To Be Secular: Reading Charles Taylor* (Eerdmans, 2014) .9-10

11 J. Barnes, *Nothing to be Frightened Of* (New York: Vintage, 2008) .1

12 Under-25s turning their backs on alcohol http://www.bbc.co.uk /news/uk-45807152

13 https://www.newstatesman.com/1997/2017/05/ cool-britannia-where-did-it-all-go-wrong

14 M. Sayers, *Disappearing Church* (Chicago: Moody Publishers, 2016)

15 This Cultural Moment, series 3, episode 9.

16 J. Welby, *Reimagining Britain* (London: Bloomsbury Continuum, 2018) .6

17 https://www.reimaginingfaith.com/content-database /marksayersroundup

18 Jeff Lucas article, *Lemmings*, in Premier Christianity Magazine, June 2019

19 T. Keller, *My Rock, My Refuge* (London: Hodder & Stoughton, 2018) .128

20 F. Chan, *Crazy Love* (Colorado Springs: David C Cook, 2008) .172

10 The Gospel

1 F. Chan, *Letters to the Church* (Colorado: David C Cook, 2018) .44

2 A. Scott, *Scattered Servants* (Colorado: David C Cook, 2018) .121

11 Encounter in the Desert

1 T. Wright, *Acts for Everyone* (London: SPCK, 2008) .127

2 D. Male & P. Weston, *The Word's Out* (Abingdon: BRF, 2019) .52

3 From the *Bible in One Year* App.

4 I. Howard Marshall, *Acts* (Leicester: IVP, 1980) .152

5 W. Neil, *The Acts of the Apostles* (London: Marshall, Morgan & Scott, 1973) .124

6 W. Barclay, *The Acts of the Apostles* (Edinburgh: The Saint Andrew Press, 1955) .71

7 P. Moore, *Straight to the Heart of Acts* (Oxford: Monarch Books, 2010) .96

8 J. Stott, *The Message of Acts* (Leicester: IVP, 1990) .162

12 Hearing the Voice of God

1 T. Wright, *Acts for Everyone, Part One* (London: SPCK, 2008) .142

2 T. Wright, *Acts for Everyone* (London: SPCK, 2008) .143

13 Mission Wider

1 E.M. Blaiklock, *Acts* (Leicester: IVP, 1959) .96

2 J. Stott, *The Message of Acts* (Leicester: IVP, 1990) .185

3 W. Barclay, *The Acts of the Apostles* (Edinburgh: The Saint Andrew Press, 1955) .90

4 O. Padilla, *The Acts of the Apostles* (London: Apollos, 2016) .169

5 F.F. Bruce, *The Book of Acts* (London: Marshall, Morgan & Scott, Ltd., 1968) .224-225

6 J.M. Boice, *Acts* (Grand Rapids: Baker Books, 1997) .172-173

7 O. Hillman, *Change Agent* (Lake Mary: Charisma House, 2011) .242

8 B. Lomenick, *The Catalyst Leader* (Nashville: Thomas Nelson Inc., 2013)

9 M. Greene, *Fruitfulness on the Frontline* (Nottingham: IVP, 2014) .201

10 https://www.premier.org.uk/News/World/Champions-League-winning-goalkeeper-shows-Christian-faith-when-celebrating

11 https://www.premierchristianity.com/Blog/Klopp-The-Christian-football-manager-who-says-there-s-more-to-life-than-winning-trophies

12 F. Laloux, *Re-inventing Organisations* (Millis: Nelson Parker, 2014)

13 M. Lucado, *Just Like Jesus* (Nashville: Thomas Nelson Publishing, 2012)

14 P. Moore, *Straight to the Heart of Acts* (Oxford: Monarch Books, 2010) .121

14 Peter's miraculous escape

1 A. Fernando, *The NIV Application Commentary: Acts* (Grand Rapids: Zondervan, 1998) .362

2 J. Boice, *Acts 'An Expositional commentary,'* (Grand Rapids: Baker Books, 2007) .210-211

3 W. Neil, *The Acts of the Apostles* (Grand Rapids: Eerdmans, 1986) .149

4 F.F. Bruce, *The Book of Acts* (London: Marshall, Morgan & Scott, Ltd., 1968) .248-249

5 I. Howard Marshall, *Acts* (Leicester: IVP, 1980) .211

6 T. Wright, *Acts for Everyone* (London: SPCK, 2012) .186

7 J. Stott, *The Message of Acts* (Leicester: IVP, 1990) .210

15 Unleashed to Unleash

1 Mark Ellis writing on www.godreports.com (September 11th, 2019

2 C. Wimber, *Wholeness* (Oxford: Lion Hudson, 2019) .105

3 Quoted from *Kingdom Unleashed* www.ncronline.org/blogs/all
   -things-catholic/uphill-journey-catholicism-china; www.telegraph.
   co.uk/news/worldnews/asia/china/10776023/china-on-course-to
   -become-worlds-most-Christian-nation-within-15-years.html

4 W. Barclay, *The Acts of the Apostles*, (Edinburgh: St Andrews Press,
   1955) .136

5 Smith Wigglesworth quote

16 Making a Difference

1 V. Frankl, *Man's Search for Meaning* (4th edition) (Boston: Beacon
   Press, 1992) .143

2 https://www.theguardian.com/society/2018/apr/05/
   young-people-have-never-been-unhappier-research-suggests

3 On Bryony Gordon's podcast *Mad World*

4 This Cultural Moment podcast, series 1 episode 3

5 D. Strange, *Plugged In* (Epsom: The Good Book Company, 2019) .17

6 R. Warren, *The Purpose Driven Life* (Grand Rapids: Zondervan,
   2006) .145

7 http://www.africa.upenn.edu/Articles_Gen/Letter_Birmingham
   .html

8 C. Calver, S. Chilcraft, *Dancing in the Dark?* (Uckfield: Spring
   Harvest, 1994) .440